Wilson County Tennessee

MINUTES OF THE COUNTY COURT

1809–1819

WPA RECORDS

Heritage Books
2024

HERITAGE BOOKS

AN IMPRINT OF HERITAGE BOOKS, INC.

Books, CDs, and more—Worldwide

For our listing of thousands of titles see our website
at
www.HeritageBooks.com

A Facsimile Reprint
Published 2024 by
HERITAGE BOOKS, INC.
Publishing Division
5810 Ruatan Street
Berwyn Heights, MD 20740

Prepared by
The Tennessee Historical Records Survey
Division of Community Service Programs
Work Projects Administration
1941

International Standard Book Number
Paperbound: 978-0-7884-8778-1

MINUTES OF COUNTY COURT VOL. 2 (or B)
1809-1819

(p 1)   DAVID McMURRY)
        vs   ) In Debt.
        SETH P. POOL   )

Pleas at the Court house in Lebanon before the worshipful the Court of pleas & quarter sessions held for the County of Wilson on the fourth Monday in March Anns Dominni 1809 and of the Independence of the United States the thirty third.

Be it remembered that heretofore (to wit) on the 4th Monday in December 1808, Seth P. Pool, was attached to answer David McMurry of a plea that he render to him four hundred and twelve dollars, which to him he owes and from him unjustly declares to his damage one hundred Dollars, whereupon the said David McMurry, by Thomas Stuart, esquire his attorney at said December Term of said Court in the year 1808 filed his decleration in the words and figures following (to wit)

State of Tennessee Wilson County December Term 1808 David McMurry Complains of Seth P. Pool in Custody, & of a plea that he render to him four hundred and twelve dollars which to him he owes and from him unjustly detains, for that where as the said Seth P. Pool, by his Certain writing obligatory made at the County aforesaid on the sixth day of January in the year one thousand eight hundred and six sealed with the seal of the said Seth P. Pool, and to the Court now shown, the date where of is the same day and year last aforesaid acknowledged himself to be justly indebted to the said David McMurry in the sum (p 2) of one thousand dollars and twelve dollars six hundred Dollars of which was to be paid after the fifth day of December next ensuing the date of said writing obligatory and the remaining four hundred and twelve were to be paid after the first day of November one thousand eight hundred and seven and the said plaintiff admits that the said Seth P. Pool, paid said six hundred dollars according as he was bound to do. But the said Seth P. Pool, tho often requested after the first day of December one thousand eight hundred and seven at the County aforesaid hath not paid said four hundred and twelve dollars nor any part thereof but the same to pay hath refused and still refuses to the damage of the said Plaintiff of one hundred dollars and there upon he brings suit &c Thos Stuart for plaintiff and at said December Term 1808 the following rule was made, plead & try at next term.

March Term 1809 the said Seth P. Pool by his attorney John E. Beck esquire puts his plea on the Docket thus payment to which is added by the plaintiffs attorney replication and issue. Whereupon at said March term 1809 Came the parties by their attornies and also a jury of good and lawful men (to wit) Henry Reed, Thomas Cypert, Archibald Davis, Mosely Harris, James Byrn, Dempsy Massey, Deveriax Wynne, Jesse Holt, Reuben Jackson, Thomas McCaplin, George Ross, John I McFerson who being elected tried and (p 3) and sworn the truth to speak upon the issue joined do say they find the defendant hath not paid the debt in the plaintiffs Decleration mention-ed amounting to four hundred and twelve dollars and assess the Executors plaintiffs damages by reason of the non payment there of to Judgement thirty two dollars and ninety cents whereupon it is considered by the court that the plaintiff recover against the defendant the sum of four hundred and twelve dollars also thirty two dollars and ninety cents his damages by the Jurors aforesaid assessed and also his costs by him about his suit in this behalf expended, and at the said March term 1809 the following memorandum was made on the docket by consent ex-ecution to be levied on the land described in the specialty in the first instance and from the said March term 1809 a writ of fire-facias essender the words and figures following levy State of Tennessee Wilson County to the sherriff of said County greetings you are hereby Commanded and, and on the back of said firi-facias see sheriffs return
See execution

L. Bradley Shff.

(p 4)   State of Tennessee Wilson County.

Pleas before the Court of Pleas and quarter sessions held for the County of Wilson at the Court house in Lebanon on the 4th Monday in March 1810 and in the 34th year of our American Independence.

JOHN DEN LESSEE OF WILLIAM TRIGG, SEN)
                Verses   ) Indictment.
WILLIAM & ELI ANDERSON, DEFT   )

William Anderson, and Eli Anderson were attached to answer John Den Lessee of Wm Trigg, Seno of a plea wherefore with force and arms he brake and entered his Close and ejected him there from, to the demage of the said John of five hundred dollars, and whereupon the said John Den by John H. Bowen esqr. his attorney, Complains for that whereas the said William Trigg Seno on the tenth day of February 1810 at the County afore-said had dismissed granted and to farm let to the said John Den six hun-dred and forty acres of land with the appurtenances situate lying and being in the County of Wilson aforesaid on the waters of Pond Lick Creek, Beginning about one hundred and sixty poles from the lick at an elm and ash thence west two hundred and ninety poles to an elm maple and oak North east Corner of Benjamin Castlemans land, thence south three hundred and fifty three poles to an Elm thence east two hundred and ninety poles to a stake, North three hundred and fifty three poles to the beginning to have and to hold the said six hundred and forty acres of land with the appurn-tenances to the said John Den and his assigns from the tenth day of February then last part until the full and end term of Ten Years, then next follow-ing and fully to be compleated and ended. (p 5) Ended by virtue of which said demise the said John Den, entered into the tenements with the appurtenances aforesaid and was there of possessed untill the said Richard Roe, afterwards (Viz) on the first day of March 1810 at the County aforesaid and with force and arms entered into the said six hundred and forty acres of land with the appurtenances in and upon the possession of the said John Doe and ejected drove out and a moved the said John Doe from his said farm, his said term not yet being expired and kept him out and still keeps him out, the said John Doe, so ejected drove out and amoved from his said farm and possession and then and there did other injuries and enormities to him the said John Doe against the peace and dignity of the State of Tennessee to the Damage of the said John five hundred dollars therefore he sues &c

John H. Bowen, for the Plff. Notice

Mr. William Anderson & Eli Anderson

     I am informed you are in possession of or Claim title to the premises in this declaration of ejectment mentioned or some part there of, and I being sued in this action as Cases a ejector and having no Claim or title to the same do advise you to appear on the forth Monday in June next at the Court to be held for the County of Wilson at the Court house by same attorney of that Court Cause your self to be made Defendant in my stead otherwise I shall suffer Judgement to be entered against me and you will be turned out of possession,

     Your loving friend Richard Roe,

Sheriff return,

     I read and delivered Copies of the written decleration and notice in ejectment to Wm and Eli Andersons' the 25th of April 1810

                    T. Bradley, Shff. W. C.

next page.

(p 6)   At June Term 1810

     The defendants Came into Court enters into the Common rule agrees to confess his entry and ouster, and on the trial rely upon the merrits only and pleads not guilty and issue.

                    Douglass, Atto.

At September Term 1810 (Continued).

At December Term 1810 Came the parties by their attornies also a jury of good and lawful men (to wit) John Impson, Frances Parmer, Jeremiah Brown, Joseph Weir, Jeremiah Taylor, John Stone, John Barllitt, Henry Howel, John Allin, John K. Wynne, William Pitman, and Thomas Donnell, who being elected tried and sworn the truth to speak upon the issue joined upon their oaths do say that the said defendants are guilty of the tresspass and ejectment aforesaid in manner and form as the plaintiff against them hath complained and assesses the ~~plaintiff~~ damages of the said plaintiff by reason of the tresspass and ejectment to six and a forth cents.

It is there fore considered by the Court that the plaintiff recover against the defendant his term yet to Come of and in the tract of land aforesaid with the appurntinances and the damages aforesaid by the jurors aforesaid ~~assessed~~ in form aforesaid and assessed also this Cost of suit in that behalf expended and the Defft. Del on Mercy &c.

Bill of Cost in the above suit viz.-

Clerks fee rent law tax and bond 2.02½ 1 Continuance 40	2.42½
5 Suponias 1.00 Judgment and record 1.00 Execution 40	2.40
Sheriff fees Executing writ and bond	2.25
Executing 5 Suponias 1.25 Declaration and notice 80	2.05
Calling Cause and empanneling Jury	.16
John Rice a witness for plff.	1.00
William Nash witness for plff.	2.00
John H. Bowen, Atto	6.25
Total costs	$18.53½

(p 7) Pleas at the Court house in Lebanon on the 4th Monday in December 1811.

ELI ANDERSON Plff.)
vs) In.
JOSEPH COLE Deft.)

This day came the parties by their attornies and a jury of good and lawful men (to wit) Philip Johnson, Henry Howel, Hugh Bradley, William Erwen, Samuel Motheral, John Firrington, Josiah Smith, James McFarling, Morris Hallum, Alexander P. Richmond, William Edwards and Benjamin Bowers, who being elected tried and sworn the truth to speak upon the issue joined, retired to considered of their verdict, and returned into Court, and say they Cannot agree.

Whereupon with the assent of the Court and the parties Consenting think Benjamin Bowers, one of the jurors is withdrawn and mistrial agreed to.

ISAAC WINSTON, Plff.)
vs) Appeal, Motion to Dismiss the appeal
JOSEPH WALSON, Deft.)

JOHN T. PICKERING, Plff.)
     vs   )   Contd. Case
ELIJAH CROSS, Deft.)

      The defendant comes into Court and Confesses judgement for sixty seven dollars and ninety three cents as by the Deft. Confessed also his costs of suit in that behalf expended and the Deft. &c.

WILLIAM LYTTLE, Plff.)
     vs   )   In Debt.
JONATHAN DOWNEY, Deft.)

      This day Came the parties by their attornies also a Jury of good and lawful men (to wit) George Smith, Hinry Davis, John Impson, Alexander Richmond, (p 8) Phillip Johnson, William Irwin, William Edwards, Jehu Ferrington, Hugh Bradley, Henry Howel, Josiah Smith, and William Anderson, who being elected tried and sworn the truth to speak upon the issue joined upon their oaths do say the Defendant hath not paid the debt in the plaintiffs Decleration mentioned amounting to one hundred and one dollars and twenty two cents, and Assess the plaintiff Damages by reason of the detention of the debts to eight Dollars and fifty cents. It is therefore Considered by the jurors aforesaid assessed also his cost about his suit in that behalf expended and the Deft. in Mercy &c.

ISHAM DAVIS, Executor of JOHN HALLUM)
     vs   )   In Case
MORRIS HALLUM)

      Contd. an affidavit of Plff.

WILLIAM EASTON & CO. Plff.)
     vs   )   Motion vs Deft. as Constable.
BENJAMIN CASTLEMAN, Deft.)

      The defendant in proper person Comes into Court and Confesses a Judgement in favor of the plaintiff for $76.85 cts. It is there-fore Considered by the Court that the plaintiff recovers against the Defendt. the sum of 76 dollars and 85 cts as by the defendant Confessed also his Cost in that behalf expended the Deft. in Mercy &c.

(p 9) Records of March Term 1812 Pleas at Lebanon in the County of Wilson before the worshipful the Court of pleas and quarter sessions for the County aforesaid on the 4th Monday in March one thousand eight hundred and twelve and of the Independence of the United States the thirty sixth.

ELI ANDERSON)
vs) In Covenant
JOSEPH COLE)

Joseph Cole was attached to answer Eli Anderson of a plea of Covenant broken to the damage of the said Eli one thousand dollars, and whereupon the said Eli Anderson by his attorney Complains For that where as the said Joseph Cole by his Certain Indenture made on the 13th day of August in the year of our Lord one thousand eight hundred and eight, between said Joseph Cole of the County of Wilson and State of Tennessee of the one part and Eli Anderson of the same County and State of the other part, Sealed with the seal of the said Joseph and to the Court now here shown bearing date the same day and year last aforesaid. It is witnessed that the said Joseph Cole for and in Consideration of the sum of seven hundred and fifty dollars, to him in hand paid by the said Eli did give grant bargain &c unto the said Eli his heirs and assigns for ever a Certain tract or parcel of land Containing 3 hundred acres, situate, lying and being in the County aforesaid on Pond Lick Creek begining at a Cedar thence South 172 poles to a walnut thence west 320 poles to an elm maple and Oak, thence North 150 poles to a stake (p 10) stake thence east 115 poles to an Ash, thence South 34 poles to a Cedar thence east eighty poles to red ash, thence North 56 poles to an elm thence east 125 poles to the begining. To have and to hold the said tract of land with the appurtinances to the said Eli Anderson, his heirs and assigns forever and the said Joseph for himself his heirs executors and administrator did Covenant to and with the said Eli Anderson, his heirs and assigns, that he would warrant and defend the said land and premises to the said Eli Anderson, his heirs and assigns forever, from the Claims of every person or persons whatsoever as by said Indenture amongst other things will more fully appear, and the said Eli in fact said that the said Joseph has not kept and performed his said Covenant in said Indenture specified on the part of the said Joseph to be kept and performed and the said Eli further in fact said that at the time of sealing and delivering said Indenture, and long before a Certain William Trigg late of the County of Sumner was and is severed of his demesne as of fee of and in Seventy two acres three fourths and ten poles of land part of said 300 acres so bargained and sold with the hereditament and appurtinances thereunto belonging by virtue of a better title than that holden by said Joseph Cole to said land part as aforesaid sold as aforesaid by the said Joseph Cole to the said Eli Anderson, by the said Indenture, said Seventy two acres three fourth and ten poles being by virtue of said Indenture in possession of said seventy two acres three fourths and ten poles of land part as aforesaid he the said William Trigg afterwards (to wit) on the day of _____

Commenced his Certain action of Tresspass and ejectment in the name of John Den his lessee against (p 11) against the said Eli Anderson in the Court of Pleas and quarter sessions for the County aforesaid in the State aforesaid, and therein the said William Trigg Complained that the said Eli Anderson had with force and arms entered into the premises aforesaid in and upon the possession of the said John Den and ejected him therefrom and kept out and still keeps said John so ejected and amoved, and that the said Eli then and there other wrongs and injures to the said Triggs lessee, to the damage of the said John Den dollars To which the said Eli Anderson by his attorney pleaded that he was not guilty of the tresspass and ejectment in said dedleration aledged in manner and form as therein stated, and for trial thereof put himself upon the County whereupon afterwards (to wit) at December term of said Court in the year 1810 it was by said Court considered that the said William Trigg's lessee should recover of the said Eli Anderson his possession aforesaid of and in and to the said Seventy two acres three fourth and ten poles of land and that thereof he should have his possession, and that the said William Trigg lessee should recover of the said Eli Anderson.

By said court adjudged for his damages and Cost in that behalf laid out and expended of the Commencement pendency and prosecution of which said action of ejectment, the said Eli Anderson, the _____ day of _____ and at sundry other times gave notice to the said Joseph Cole, and the said Eli further in fact saith that the said William Trigg by virtue of his title and the recovery aforesaid entered into the said seventy two acres three fourths and ten poles of land part of said 300 so granted bargained &c by said Joseph Cole to the said Eli Anderson and said Eli from such part aforesaid totally expelled and amoved and was and still is in possession thereof and withholds the possession of the same from the said Eli Anderson, which said part and parcel the said Eli (p 12) Eli avers is the same and is part of the said 300 acres granted bargained and sold as aforesaid, by the said Joseph Cole, to the said Eli Anderson and farther that the said Joseph the said seventy two acres, three fourths and ten poles of land part as aforesaid of the said 300 acres has not warranted and defended against the claim of every person or persons what so ever, as by the said Indenture is intended but the same to do has and still does refuse to the damage of the said Eli one thousand dollars.

Douglass, Atto.

And at the September Term of said Court in the year one thousand eight
hundred and eleven the said defendant by Jesse Wharton his attorney comes
and defends the force and injury where and when it shall behove him and says
that he has not broken his Covenant as plaintiff is declairing hath eledged,
and there of he puts himself upon the County and the plaintiff also, and the
said cause was Continued untill December Term 1811 at which time Came the
parties by their attornies and a jury of good and lawful men to wit. Phillip
Johnson, Henry Howel, Hugh Bradly, William Erwin, Samuel Motheral, Jehu
Ferrington, Josiah Smith, James McFarling, Morris Hallum, Alexander P. Richmond,
William Edwards and Benjamin Bowers, who being elected tried and sworn the
truth to speak upon the issue joined retired to consider of their verdict, and
returned into Court and say the cannot agree, whereupon with the assent of the
Court and the parties Consenting thereto Benjamin Bowers one of the jurors is
withdrawn and a miss trial agreed to, and at March term the first above mentioned Came the parties by their attornies and also a jury of good and lawful men
to wit Samuel W. Sherrill, Andrew Foster, Arther Dew, John Harpole, William H.
Peace, James B. Lockhart, Reuben Bullard, Hesekiah Cartwright, Thomas Leech,
Robert Bumpass, Samuel Stuart, and Robert Foster, who being elected tried and
sworn the truth (p 13) to speak upon the issue joined upon their oaths do
say the defendant hath not kept and performed his Covenant with the said plaintiff as in pleading he hath eledged and assesses the plaintiffs damages by reason there of to six hundred dollars. It is there fore considered by the
Court that the said Eli Anderson, recover of the said Joseph Cole, the damages
aforesaid by the jury aforesaid in form aforesaid assessed and also his cost
by him about his suit in this behalf expended and that the said Defendant &c.

From which Judgement the defendant prays and appeal to the next Circuit
Court to be holden for the County of Wilson on the fourth Monday in September
next, which is granted and thereupon the said Joseph intered into bond with
Charles Blalock and Beverly Williams, his securities in the sum of two
thousand dollars for the prosecution of said appeal with effect or in Case of
failure, the payment of such damages and Costs as may be awarded against him,
and by Jessee Wharton his attorney files reasons for same and Bill of Costs:

Clerks fee Capias and bond 1.40 order of Survey 25.	
Jury and Mistrial .40 cts. two Continuances 80 cts five	
suponia 100 cts. Judgement 100 cts appeal and Transcript	$6.25
1.40 including seal Law tax 62½ cts.	.62½
Sherriff fees	3.00
Atto. Douglass	6.25
Benjamin Hooker a witness	4.50 cts.
Benjn. Newls.	4.50 cts.
Samuel Allin	4.50 cts.
William Nash	3.00¼ cts.
John K. Wynne	4.50 cts Richd.
Ramsey	1.00 cts.
Dolls.	38.18-3/4

(p 14)   Records of March Term 1813.

Pleas before the Court of pleas and quarter sessions held at the Court house in the town of Lebanon for the County of Wilson on the first Monday in March 1813 & 37th year of American Independence.

JOHN BRICE, Plff.)
vs   ) Appeal
JOSEPH COLE, Deft.)

State of Tennessee Wilson County.

To any lawful officer to execute and return.

Summon Joseph Cole, to appear before some Justice of the peace for said County to answer the Complaint of John Brice, in a plea of debt forty two dollars due by note given under my hand this 8th day of February 1813.

John Hannah, J. P.

Executed and returned Febry. the 13th 1813.

G. H. Hannah

February the 13th 1813 Judgement is found against the defendant for twenty four dollars ninety four cents with cost of suit.

Ransom Gwyn,

JOHN BRUCE, Plff.)
vs.   ) March Term 1813
JOSEPH COLE, Deft.) Appeal

The Defendant by his attorney moved the Court to quash the warrant and proceedings in this Case had before the justice of the peace which motion was over ruled by the Court and there upon Came the parties by their attornies and also a jury (p 15) of good and lawful men (to wit) Joseph Berry, James Sinclair, James Bonds, Alexander Wetherspoon, Benjamin Bowers, John Clemmons, James Turner, William Lawrence, John T. Cooksey, John Allin, William Adams, and Giles Bowers, who being elected tried and sworn the bruth to speak upon the issue joined upon their oaths do say they find for the plaintiff twenty one dollars debt and assess his damage to four dollars for the detention there of. It is therefore considered by the Court that the plaintiff recover of the Defendant his debt and damages by the Jury assessed also his Costs about his suit expended from which Judgement the Defendant prayes an appeal, filed his reason and entered into bond as the law directs with James Cross and George Mechie, his securities upon which an appeal is granted the Defendant to the next Circuit Court to be holden at the Court house in Lebanon on the first Monday in September next.

Bill of Costs in the above Case:
Constable G. H. Hannah, executing Warnt. $ .50
Law tax 62½ and Judgement 100   1.62½
Attorney   1.25
                                                             $4.77½

State of Tennessee) J. John Allcorn
     Wilson County   Clerk &c

(p 16) Records of June Term 1813.

Pleas at the Court house in Lebanon in the County of Wilson and State of Tennessee before the worshipful Court of pleas and quarter sessions on the third Monday in June Anno Domini 1813 and 37th year of American Independence.

WHITE & JO H. COUN Plff.
vs
BRITTAIN DRAKE, Deft. } In Debt.

Brittain Drake was attached to answer White & Jo H. Coun of a plea that he rendered to them their one hundred and five dollars and thirty cents - which to them he owes and from them unjustly aclaims &c.

Whereupon the said White & Jo H. Coun by their attorney at March Term 1813 made profect in open Court and ayes was had of the writing obligatory on which said action was founded which was in the words and figures following For $105.30 H.N.A. one day after date I promise to pay White & Jo H. Coun, as assigns the sum of one hundred and five dollars thirty cents for his open account and Jesse Boon and Brittian Drake, open asct. for value received witness my hand and seal this 20th June 1812,

Test:
John W. Vaughan) Brittain Drake,

And thereupon the said Brittian at the term last above mentioned by his attorney John E. Beck, pleaded on the docket thus payment Shff Office* on which there was replication and issue.

And now at this term (to wit) the term first above mentioned Came the parties by their attornies and thereupon Came a jury of honest and lawful men (to wit) George Swingley, William Crawford, John Doak, Edmund Crutcher, Thomas Bradley, James Crawford, (p 17) Beverly Peace, William Jones, William Tigue, and Richard Hancock, who being elected tried and sworn the truth to speak upon the issue joined between the parties upon their oaths do say the Defendant has not paid the said debt of one hundred and five dollars and thirty Cents as in pleading he hath alledged find no set and assess damages by the reason of the non payment there of to six dollars and thirty cents, It is there fore considered by the Court that the said plaintiff recover of the defendant the debt aforesaid of one hundred and five dollars and thirty Cents to gether with the damages afis by the Jury aforesaid in form aforesaid assessed amounting in the whole to one hundred and eleven dollars and sixty cents and also his costs by him about his suit in this behalf expunded and that said Deft. &c. and thereupon said Brittain Drake, prays an appeal to the next Circuit Court to be held for the County of Wilson on the first Monday in September next and interest into bond conditioned as the law directs with Jeremiah Tucker, and Leonard H. Sims, his securities and filed reasons for the same.

Bill of Cost.

Writ law tax & bond 2.02½ cts.   )
Judgement 1.00   )
Copy record & seal 1.40   )   4.42½
Sheriff Executing writ & bond   1.25
Atto. Williams & Shelly   2.50
    8.22½

Judgement 22nd June 1813 for $111.60 cts.

Clerk Certificate

(p 18) Records of June Term 1813.

HARMON A HAYS, Plff.   )
    vs   )   Attach &
WYATT WILKERSON, Deft.   )

Now at this Term June 1813, Came the plaintiff by his attorney Harry L. Douglass and the Deft. Wyatt Wilkerson altho solemnly called Came not nor is defence made.

It is therefore Considered by the Court that the said Harmon A. Hays recover of the said Defendant Wyat Wilkerson, his debt of one hundred and forty Dollars, to gether with nine dollars and ten cents damages & also his Costs by him about his suit in this behalf expended and that the land levied on behold to satisfy said debt Damages & Costs & see page _____ a full record of all the proceedings.

(p 19) State of Tennessee Wilson County Lit.

Pleas before the Court of pleas and quarter sessions held for the County Wilson at the Court house in the town of Lebanon on the 4th Monday in December A. D. 1812 and XXXVII years of American Independence.

THOMAS AMES, Plaintiff)
                 vs   )   In Covenant
DANIEL CHERRY, Defendant)

Whereas a writ issue thus.

State of Tennessee To the Sheriff of Wilson greeting you are hereby Commanded to take the body of Daniel Cherry if to be found and him safely keep so that you have him before the justices of our Court of pleas and quarter Sessions to be held for the County of Wilson at the Court house in the town of Lebanon on the third Monday in March next this and there to answer Thomas Ames of a plea of Covenant broken to his damage one thousand dollars herein fail not, and have you then this writ.

Witness John Allcorn, Clerk of our said Court at office this 4th Monday in December A. D. 1812 and XXXVII years of American Independence.

John Allcorn   Clk.

I acknowledge my self the above plaintiffs security in writ with effect on payment of all Cost & Damages incident in failure there of witness my hand and seal this 1st day of March 1813.

Jethro Hardey

Issued the 1st March 1813 Came to hands the same day issue Executed the 3rd March 1813.

W. Woodward   D.S.

(p 20) At March term 1813 Came the plaintiff by William Williams, Esq.
his attorney and filed his Declaration in the following words & figures
(to wit)

Wilson County March term 1813 Thomas Ames, by his attorney Complains
of Daniel Cherry in Custody &c of a plea of Covenant broken for that whereas the
said Daniel on the 11th day of January 1809 at Martin County viz. at Lebanon
in the County aforesaid made his certain writing obligatory of that day and
date and here produced to the Court which witnesseth that the Defendant had
received of said plaintiff a transfer of a Military land warrant for six
hundred and forty acres of the No. 160 issued in the name of the heir John
Ames the only heir binding him self said defendant to locate said warrant and
have the same refined into land and granted at his own expense and after it
is so granted to make or cause to be made a deed of Conveyance to two hundred
Acres of said land, to said plaintiff his heirs executors administrators &c,
and said plaintiff saith said Defendant hath not kept and performed his
Covenant aforesaid but hath broken it in the that he has not located said
warrant and refined it into land and Caused it to be granted at his own expense,
and made a deed of Conveyance to said plaintiff for two hundred acres of land.
Agreeable to the written Convenant to the plaintiff Damage one thousand dollars,
and there upon his bring suit.

Will Williams P. atty.

At said March term 1813, a rule of Court was made on the appearance Docket thus.
(p 21) At June term following stands entered on the trial Docket (thus) non.
enfregit Conventions performance Condition Replecition and issue.

Continued until next term.

At September Term 1813 Came the parties by their attorneys also a
Jury of good and lawful men (to wit) Joseph Berry, David Bradley, John
Merritt, William Wortham, Edward Harris, Henry Rice, Humphry Dennelson,
William Edwards, George Tucker, Clem Jennings, Silas Chapman, and John Bone,
who being elected tried and sworn the truth to speak upon the issue joined
upon these oaths do say the defendant hath not kept and performed his
Covenant with the said plaintiff as in pleading he hath alledged, and assess
the plaintiff damages by reason of his non performance of the same, to six
hundred dollars.

It is there fore considered by the Court that the said Ames recover
of said Cherry six hundred Dollars the Damages aforesaid by the jury aforesaid
in form aforesaid assessed and also his Cost by him about his suit in this behalf expended and there upon the said Defendant prayeth an appeal to the next
Circuit Court which is granted and the said Cherry enters into bond with Eli
Cherry and John Hill his securities &c filed names &c.

Bill of cost viz.

Suit Law tax and prosecution bond	2.02½
One Subpoena .20	.20
One Continuance .40	.40
Judgement and record	1.00
Appeal & Bond 1.40	1.40
Sheriff fee arrest & Bond	1.25
Executing 2 suponias	.50
Calling & empanneling Jury----	
Picket Stone a witness for plaintiff	3.50
Amt. Cost $12.93½	$12.93½

(p 22) Pleas at the Court house in Lebanon in the State of Tennessee before the Court of pleas and quarter Sessions held for the County of Wilson on the third Monday in September A. D. 1813 & 38th Year of American Independence-

JOHN DOE lessee of HENRY BAILEY, Plft.)
            vs   )   In Ejectments
PHILLIP SMART & NICHOLAS SWINGLEY, Deft.)

       Be it remembered that here to fore (to wit) at December Term of said Court in the year 1812 Phillip Smart was attached to answer John Doe lessee of Henry Bailey of a plea of tresspass & ejectment with force and arms to his damage five hundred dollars whereupon the said John by H. L. Douglass his attorney filed his decleration in the words and figures following, (to wit) Wilson County Court &c John Doe by his attorney Complains of Richard Roe in custody &c for that whereas Henry Baily on the 1st day of September 1812 had levied & demeased to the said John one Cottage and one hundred Acres of land situate in the County of Wilson aforesaid on the head waters of Cedar Lick Creek granted to the said Henry by patent from the Seals of Tennessee No. 2874 dated the fifth day of February in the year 1811 begining at a black gum & black Oak on Thomas Blair southern boundary line thence south 126 poles to a dogwood & poplar thence East 126 poles to two hickories on the ridge between Pond Lick Creek and Cedar Lick Creek thence North 126 poles to a white oak & post oak thence west 126 poles passing said Blairs south east corner and with his south boundary line to the begining with the appurtances to have to hold to the said John and his assigns from the said first day of September to the full end and term of ten years thence next ensuing & fully to be Compleated and ended by virtue of which said demses the said John Doe entered into said Cottage and land with the appurtenances and was there of possessed and the said John being so possessed there of the said Richard afterwards (to wit) the same (p 23) same day and year first above mentioned with force and arms entered into the said Cottage and land with the appurtenances demesed to the said John in form aforesaid for the term aforesaid which is not yet expired and ejected the said John there from and other wrongs and injuries to the said John Doe did against the peace and dignity of the State, and to the damage of the said John five hundred dollars and therefore he brings suit.

                                         Douglass atto. for Plft.

Mr. Phillip Smart

Sir   I am informed that you are in possession of or Claim title to the premises in the above decleration of ejectment mentioned or to some part these of and I being sued in this action as Casual ejector and having no claim or title to the same do advise you to appear at the next Court of pleas & quarter sessions to be held for Wilson County at the Court house in Lebanon on the fourth Monday in December next, then and there by a rule to be made of the same Court to cause yourself to be made Defendant in my stead otherwise I will suffer Judgement to be entered against me & you will be turned of possession

       Septm. 1812   Yours
                                        Richard Roe

And at said December Term Nicholas Swingley on Motion is admitted as codefendant with the tenant in possession, agrees to confess lease entry and auster and on the trial to rely on the title only, and pleads not guilty & thereupon issue is joined and the said cause was continued from term to term until June Term 1812 at which time Came the parties by their attorney (p 24) attornies and there upon Came a Jury of good and lawful men (to wit) Ebenezar Hern, John Fakes, Samuel Gray, James McAdow, James Welch, William H. Peace, John Simpson, John Harpole, Samuel Motheral, Samuel Calhoun, Deveraux Jarratt, and Thomas Smith who being elected tried and sworn the truth to speak upon the issue joined upon their oaths do say the defendants are guilty of the tresspass & ejectment in manner & form as the plaintiff in declaring hath alledged & assess his damages by reason there of to one cent.

It is there fore considered by the Court that the plaintiff recover of said Defendant his term yet to come of in and to the premises with the appurtenances in his declaration mentioned and also the damages aforesaid by the jury aforesaid in leven aforesaid aforesaid assessed together with his costs by him about his suit in this behalf expended- and on motion of the Defendant by his attorney a new trial is granted to be had thereon at the next term of this Court. And now at this term to wit. the term first above mentioned Came the parties by their attornies and thereupon came a jury of good and lawful men (to wit) - William New, Daniel Benthal, Obediah G. Finley, Henry Cooke, Thomas Wooldridge, Samuel Motheral, Beverly Williams, John Alsup, Clem Jennings, Ship a Puckett, William Thomas, and Eleasor Prowine, who being elected tried and sworn the truth to speak upon the issue joined upon their oaths do say the Defendant is not guilty of the tresspass and ejectment in manner and form as the plaintiff is declaring hath alledged It is therefore considered by the Court that the said Defendant go hence with out day and recover against the plaintiff his Costs by him about his defence in this behalf expended whereupon the said plaintiff prays an appeal to the Circuit Court next (p 25) next to be holden for said County which after entering into bond with Charles Blalock his security & filing reasons for the same is by the Court is here granted.

Bill of Cost.
Writ Law tax & bond 2.02½ rule admiting defendant .24)
Jury & new trial .40 cts. 5 sups. 100 cts Judgement &)
record 1.00 appeal 1.60   ) $5.62½
Sheriff executing writ and taking bond   1.25
Serving Copy declaration .80 executing 9 subponeas
.25 .. 2.50   4.55
Charles Blalock a witness 5 days   2.50
James Mays a witness 5 days   2.50
Joseph Cole a witness 3 days   1.50
John Doak a witness six days one Sureyor   5.00
Sept. Term 1813.
William P. Burnet, a witness 5 days   2.50
Nancy Chandler a witness for Deft. 4 days   2.00
John Doak a witness 5 days one Surveyer   4.50

- Transcript made out -
and sent up to the
Circuit Court

(p 26) At a Court of pleas & quarter sessions held for the   on Monday the 21st March 1814 and present the worshipful Christopher Cooper, Walter Carruth, George Clark, James Cross, Deveraux Wynne, Isaac Winston, Samuel Cannon, and William McClain, Esquire who took their seats & proceeded to business

Tuesday the 22nd 1814.

WILLIAM BLOODWORTHS Lessee Plff. & Others)
vs   ) Indictment
JAMES CRAWFORD, Deft.   )

  This day came the plaintiff by his attorney & the Defendant being solemnly Called cannot muther is any defence made for him. It is therefore considered by the Court that the plaintiff recover against the defendant their term yet to come of and in the premises & appurtenances aforesaid. Also his costs of suit in this behalf expended &c. 1

SHADRACK GRIGG Plff.)
vs   ) Appeal Continued   2
JOHN GREGORY Deft.   )

GEORGE DONNELL Lessee Plft.)
vs   ) In ejectment -
JAMES SEATT, Deft.   ) Continued for the absence of Sampson
) Williams.

JAMES WALLACE, Lessee Plff.)
vs.   ) In Ejectment - Continued
EDMOND CRUTCHER, Deft.   )

ELIAZER PROVINE Lessee Plff.)
vs.   ) In Ejectment.
WILLIAM THOMAS Deft.   )

  This day came the parties by their attornies also a jury of good and lawful men (to wit) James Turner, John Beard, Perry Taylor, Richard Ligan, John Curry, Edwards Hunter.

(p 27) County of Wilson in the town of Lebanon 38th year of American Independence Bird Smith, Arther Dew, Marten Talley, Beverly Williams, Henning Pace, William Howard, who being elected tried and sworn the truth to speak upon the issue joined upon their oaths do say the defendant is guilty of the tresspass and ejectment in manner & form as the plaintiff in declairing against him hath alledged and assess the plaintiff damages to six and a fourth cents - It is there fore Considered by the Court that the plaintiff recover against the Defendant his term yet to come of and in the premises with the appurtinances aforesaid together with his damages aforesaid by the jury in form aforesaid assessed also his cost by him about his suit in this be-half expended, and on motion it is ordered that he thereof have his possession &c.

L. & J. ALEXANDER   Plft.)
       vs.   )   Certiorari
EDITH CAMPBELL   Deft.)

      Continued by the Plaintiff on account of A. McIntire a witness being in the Army.

JOHN CARTWRIGHT   Plft.)
       vs.   )   Appeal Cont. by Consent.
JOHN TELFORD   Deft.)

JOHN HART   Plft.)
       vs.   )   In Debt
LEFEVER STREET   Deft.)

      This day came the parties by their attornies also a jury of good and lawful men (to wit) John Beard, Harmon A. Hays, David Keys, Aaron Stuart, Thomas Collins, Thomas Carver, John Curry, Perry Taylor, Edwards Hunter, Richard Ligan, Joel Echols and (p 28) and Thomas Ames who being elected tried and sworn the truth to speak upon the issue joined upon their oaths do say the defendant hath not kept and performed his Covenant with the said plaintiff but hath broken the same and assess damage by reason there of to one hundred and twenty two dollars and forty two and a half cents. It is there fore Considered by the Court that the said plaintiff recover against the Defendant the said sum of one hundred & thirty two dollars forty two and a half cents as by the jury aforesaid in form aforesaid assessed also his Cost of suit in this be-half expended & the deft. in Mercy &c.

      Stephen Roberts a witness for the Plaintiff 2 days.

      2 days 24 miles traveling & 2 ferriges.

WILLIAM PATTERSON   Plft.)
       vs.   )   In Debt.
ARMSTEAD STUBLEFIELD   Deft.)

      This day came the parties by their attornies also a jury of good and lawful men (to wit) James Turner, John Baird, Perry Taylor, Richard Ligan, John Curry, Edward Hunter, Martin Tally, Obediah G. Finley, James Godfry, Warner Lambeth, Isaac Williams, and Abner Wason, who being elected tried and sworn the truth to speak upon the issue joined upon their oaths do say they find the Defendant hath not paid the debt in the plaintiffs specialty mentioned the balance of the debt and interest amounting to four hundred and fifty seven dollars & twenty five cents. It is therefore considered by the Court that the said Plaintiff recover against the defendant the said sum of (p 29) four hundred fifty seven Dollars and twenty five Cents for his balance of debt & damages by way of interest as by the Jury aforesaid in form aforesaid assessed also his Cost about his suit in this behalf expended & the debt in Mercy &c.

WILLIAM PATTERSON, Plaintiff)
      vs   ) In Debt.
ARMSTEAD STUBLEFIELD, Deft.)

This day came the parties by their attornies also a jury of good and lawful men (to wit) James Turner, John Baird, Perry Taylor, Richard Ligon, John Curry, Edward Hunter, Martin Tally, Obediah G. Finley, James Godfrey, Warner Lambeth, Isaac Williams, and Abner Wason, who being elected tried and sworn the truth to speak upon the issue joined upon their oaths do say they find the defendant hath not kept and performed the conditions as in pleading he hath alledged and hath not paid the debt in the plaintiffs specialty mentioned of nine hundred and sixty eight Dollars and assess the damages assationed by the detention of said debt to seventy two dollars & sixty Cents.

It is therefore Considered by the Court that the Plaintiff recover against the said Defendant the sum of Nine hundred and sixty eight dollars for his debt also seventy two dollars sixty Cents damages as by the jury aforesaid in form aforesaid assessed also his Cost of suit in this behalf expended & the Deft. in Mercy &c.

A deft. Term 1813
Enoch Dange a witness proved 2 days 87 miles.

At March term 1814.
John O'Neal a witness proved 2 days.

(p 30)
JOHN BONNER, Plaintiff)
      vs.   ) Appeal
SETH P. POOL, Defendant)

This day came the parties by their attornies also a jury of good and lawful min (to wit) James Turner, John Baird, Perry Taylor, Richard Ligan, John Curry, Edward Hunter, Marlin Tally, Obediah G. Finley, James Godfry, Warner Lambeth, Isaac Williams, & Abner Wasson, who being elected tried and sworn the truth to speak upon the issue joined upon their oaths do say they find for the Defendant.

It is therefore Considered by the Court that the Defendant go hence without day and recover against the Plaintiff his Costs about his defence in this behalf expended George Dillard, a witness proved 6 days.

THOMAS DONNELL, Plft.)
      vs.   ) Certiorari
I. MILLER, Deft.)

It is agreed this Cause shall be refered to Walter Carruth, Samuel Cannon, John Payton, and James Williams, if they dont agree they are to call in an umpire, and their award to be the Judgement of this Court the award to be returned to next Court.

SAMUEL ALLIN, Plft.)
vs) In Debt.
JNO W. LUMPKINS, Deft.)

The Defendant on this day Comes into Court, withdraws his plea & confesses the plaintiffs debt the balance due on the plaintiffs specialty amounting to two hundred and twenty six dollars and twenty five Cents with nineteen dollars seventy four Cents Interest thereon.

It is therefore Considered by the Court that the Plaintiff aforesaid recover against said Deft. his debt & interest aforesaid Confessed amounting to 285.99 cts. Also his Cost of suit &c.

(p 31) HUMPHRY DONELSON, Plft.)
vs) In Ejectment
GEORGE SMITH, Deft.)

This Cause is Continued until next Court It is ordered by the Court that William Seawell be appointed to survey the premises in dispute and return two fair plats thereof to next Court.

Jas. Mullherrin a witness proved two days 46 miles & two ferreges.

BENJAMIN NICHOLS, Plft.)
vs.) In Ejectment
BENJAMIN HOOKER, Deft.)

This day came the parties by their attornies & also a Jury of good and lawful men (to wit) Henry Bailey, George Harpole, Edward Harris, Boothe Melone, William Bettes, Marshall Piper, Richard Hankins, John Hallum, Rowland Sutton, Joseph Castleman, David Moser, & Isham Wynne, who being elected tried and sworn the truth to speak upon the issue joined upon their oaths do say the Defendant is guilty of the tresspass and ejectment in manner and form as the Plaintiff in declaring against him hath allegded and assess the plaintiff damages to six and a fourth Cents. It is therefore Considered by the Court that the said Plaintiff recover against the defendant his term yet to come of and in the premises with the appurtenances aforesaid in the Plaintiff declaration mentioned together with the damages aforesaid by the jury in form aforesaid assesssed also his costs by him about his suit in this behalf expended.

John Hannah, a witness proved one days attendance.
Will Nash, witness 3 days & 34 miles.

(p32) JOHN DEW Lessee of Plft.)
WILLIAM LYTLE)
vs) In Ejectment.
SAMUEL MILLER)

This day Came the plaintiff by his attorney and the defendant altho solemnly called came not nor is defence made. It is therefore considered by the Court that the said John Dew, recover of the said Samuel Miller, his term to Come of & in the premises with the appurtenances aforesaid and also his Cost by him about his suit in this behald expended & that thereof he have his possession.

DUNCAN STUART, Plft.)
vs) In Debt.
JAMES RATHER, Deft.)

This day came the parties by their attornies and the Defendant in proper person with draws his plea & confeses the plaintiffs action against him, and says he is indebted to the plaintiff two hundred dollars with twelve dollars sixty seven cents interest.

If is therefore considered by the Court that the said plft. recover against the said defendant the said sum of two hundred dollars for his debt also twelve dollars & sixty seven Cents interest there as by the Defendant Confessed also the Cost of suit in this behalf expended &c.

(p 33) SAMUEL CANNON, Admr. of Plft. JAMES CANNON, Decd.)
vs.) In Debt
WILLIAM MANN, & JOHN MARSHALL, Deft.)

The Defendants by their attornies Comes into Court & withdraws their pleas, and Confeses the Judgment according to specialty with interest amounting to five hundred & thirty dollars thirty seven and a half Cents. It is there fore Considered by the Court that the Plaintiff recover against the defendants the sum of five hundred & thirty Dollars thirty seven and a half Cents as by the said Defendants Confessed Also his Costs about his suit in that behalf expended & the debts &c.

ROGER QUARLES Plft.)
vs) Attachment
RICHARD HOPKINS, Deft.)

The defendant being solemnly called and failing to appear on motion of the plaintiff by his attorney Judgement is intered by default is entered by default awarding to specialty amounting to thirty five Dollars, also Cost of suit, this entry was Crossed in Mistake.

JOHN ECHOLS Assign of
DEVERAUSE JARRETT   Plft.)
vs) In Debt.
BENJAMIN WRIGHT & JOHN DEW Deft.)

The Defendants by their attornies Comes into Court and Confeses the Plaintiffs actions withdrawing (p 34) withdraws their pleas & confesses Judgment according to the Plaintiffs specialty to the Court has shown amounting to one hundred and five dollars also the Cost about this suit expended It is therefore Considered by the Court that the said Plaintiff recover against the said defendant the said sum of one hundred and five dollars the debt and interest in the Plaintiffs specialty mentioned.

Also his Cost of suit in this behalf expended & that he have his executor &c.

GEORGE TUCKER Plft.　)
　　　vs　　　　　　) 　In Debt.
GEO. & Wm HALLUM Deft.)

　　　The Defendants by their attorney Comes into Court & withdraws the pleas & Confeses Judgt. according to specialty with interest. It is therefore ordered by the Court that the Plft. recover against the Defendants the debt in his specialty mentioned amounting to one hundred and thirty three dollars and twenty eight Cents for his debt also three dollars sixty six Cents interest thereon - Also Cost of suit in this behalf expended.

JEREMIAH TUCKER Guardian Plft.)
　　　vs　　　　　　　　　　　　)
GEORGE & MORRIS HALLUM Deft.)

　　　The defendants by their attornies with draws the pleas and confesses Judgement according to specialty with interest amounting to one hundred and sixty two dollars and seven Cents. It is therefore Considered by the Court that the plaintiff recover against the Deft. the sum of 162. 7 Cents as by Defts. Confessed also his Costs of suit.

(p 35)　THOMAS WILSON & CO. Plaintiff)
　　　　　　vs　　　　　　　　　　　) 　In Debt.
OBEDIAH SPRADLEY, Deft. Administrator)
　of L. ECHOLS　　　　　　　　　　　)

　　　Pleas withdrawn and Judgement Confessed according to specialty with interest thereon. It is there fore Considered by the Court that the Plaintiff recover against the said Defendant sixty one dollars and thirty two Cents for the debt in the Plaintiffs specialty mentioned with fourteen dollars sixty eight Cents interest due thereon amounting in the whole to seventy six dollars Also his Costs about his suit in this be-half expended & the Deft. in Mercy &c.

WILLIAM LYTLE JR Plft.)
　　　vs　　　　　　　　) 　In Debt.
ANTHONY WINSTON Deft.)

　　　This day Came the parties by their attornies also a Jury of good and lawful men to wit Henry Baily, George Harpole, Edward Harris, Boothe Melone, William Bettis, Marshall Piper, Richard Hankins, John Hallum, Rowland Sutton, Joseph Castleman, Daniel Moser, and Isham Wynne, who being elected tried and sworn the truth to speak upon the issue Joined upon their oaths do say the Deft. hath not paid the Debt in the plaintiffs specialty mentioned as in pleading he hath alledged and assess the damage ascertained by the detentioned of the Plft. debt. to sixty four dollars & fifty Cents.

　　　It is therefore Considered by the Court that the Plft. for his debt $511 Damages 64.50 cts & the Deft. &c.

(p 36) THOMAS RICHMOND   Plft.)
                    vs   )   Motion on an Execution
       SAMUEL McKEE   Deft.)   in the following words to wit

  State of Tennessee Wilson County to any lawful officer, to execute
& return you are hereby Commanded that of the goods and Chattels lands and
tenements of Samuel McKee if to be found in your County you make the sum of
eighty five dollars and fifty Cents to satisfy a Judgement that Thomas
Richmond obtained against said McKee before me this day given under my hand
the 26th day of February 1814.

         James Richmond, J. P.

  Upon which execution the following returns are endorsed, no personal
property found by me.
        J. Bond, Const.   Febry 28th
1814 Levied on 40 acres of land February the 28th 1814 whereon Samuel McKee
now lives.
        J. Bond, Const.

  It is therefore Considered by the Court that the said 40 acres of
land so levied on be Condemned and sold to satisfy the Plaintiffs of Eighty
five dollars and fifty Cents also the Cost accuring on this motion and that
the Clerk issue an order of sale directed to the sheriff &c.

NOTLEY MADDOX   Plft.)
             vs   )   Motion on an Executor.
SAMUEL McKEE   Deft.)

  It is ordered by the Court that the 40 acres of land whereon the
said Defendant lives be Condemned and sold for the benefit of the Plaintiff
Judgement and Cost aquetile to the Constables return &c.

(p 37) LAWRENCE SYPERT   Plft.)
                     vs   )
       SAMUEL McKEE   Deft.)

  Motion on an execution in the words & figures following State of
Tennessee Wilson County To any lawful officer you are Commanded to execute
the goods and Chattels lands & tenements of Samuel McKee if to be found in
your County or as much as will make the sum of thirty six dollars and twenty
five Cents with legal Costs to satisfy a Judgement that Laurence Sypert
assignee of Notley Maddox obtained against him given under my hand this 18th
day of February.

        Jas. Johnson, J. P.

Upon said execution was the following endorsment to wit. No Personal property of the Defendant to be found by me. February 25th 1814 levied on forty acres of land where the said McKee now lives.

Jerh. Tucker, Const.

on the Motion of the said plaintiff It is Considered by the Court that the said forty acres of land so levied on be Condemned and sold for the benefit of said Judgement and Costs, and that an order of sale issue.

JAMES RICHMOND Plft.)
        vs   )   Motion on an Execution
SAMUEL McKEE   Deft.)

It is ordered by the Court 40 acres of land levied on as the property of the defendant be Condemned and sold to satisfy the balance due the plaintiffs Execution and that an order of sale issue.

(p 38)   JOHN DEN Lessee of Plft.)
         JAMES WHITSETT, Lessee   )
                vs   )   In Ejectment.
         ANDREW HAYS, Deft.   )

This day came the plaintiff by his attorney and the defendant tho solemnly Called Came not, nor is any defence made.

It is therefore Considered by the Court that the said John Den recover of the said Andrew Hays his term to come of and in the premises with the appnutences aforesaid, also his Costs about his suit in this be-half expended and that things he have in his possession.

ROGER QUARLES Plaintiff)
        vs   )   Attachment
RICHARD HOPKINS Deft.   )

This day Came the plaintiff by his attorney and the Defendant being solemnly Called and failed to appear. And it appearing to the Court that this Cause has been continued six months under the law It is therefore Considered by the Court that the Plaintiff recover against the Defendant the sum of thirty five Dollars the sum Complained of in the attachment for his Debt.

Also his cost of suit, and that the two hundred & sixty seven acres of land levied on by the attachment be sold for the satisfaction of the said debt and Costs aforesaid and that an order of sale issue to sell the same.

NOTE: Page 39 blank in original.

(p 40)   Moss

(p 40) Pleas before the Court of pleas and quarter sessions held for the County of Wilson in the State of Tennessee at the Court house in Lebanon on the 4th Monday in September 1812 and of the Independence of the United States the 37th.

HARMON A. HAYS   Plft.)
        vs   )   Attd. &
WYAT WILKERSON   Deft.)

Wilson County   )
       State of Tennessee)   This day James Davis agent for Harmon A. Hays appeared before me James S. Rawlings an acting Justice of the peace for said County and made oath that a Certain Wyat Wilkerson, on bond stands justly indebted to said Hays the sum of one hundred and forty three dollars and twenty five Cents principal & interest and that the said Wyat Wilkerson is not a Citizen of this state - therefore the ordinary prosess of law cannot be served upon him & prays an attachment as given under his hand this 19th Sept. 1812.

                                            James Davis, J. P.

Sworn to & Subscribed the date above.

                                            James S. Rawlings, J. P.

Wilson County   )
       State of Tennessee)   To any lawful officer whereas James Davis appeared before me James S. Rawlings an acting Justice (p 41) for said County and made oath as agent for Harmon A. Hays, that a Certain Wyat Wilkerson, was justly indebted said Hays one hundred and forty three dollars twenty five Cents and that the said Wilkerson, appears to be not an inhabitant of this State and prays an attachment in this County & prays an attachment in this County and gave bond and security according to law.

       You are hereby Commanded that of the goods and Chattels lands & tenements of Wyat Wilkerson if found in your County you attach so much thereof as will make the sum of one hundred and forty three dollars and twenty five Cents, and all legal Costs to satisfied the above Complaint and such property when attached safely keep & secure - and have you tried this suit with your proceedings before the justices of our next County Court to be further dealt with as the law directs. As given under my hand this 19th Sept. 1812.

                                            Jas. S. Rawlings, J. P.

Wilson County   )
       State of Tennessee)   We are held & firmly bound unto Wyat Wilkerson, in the sum of two hundred and eighty six dollars & fifty Cents paid on Condition that said James Davis as agent for Harmon A. Hays doth with effect lawfully prosecute an attachment against said Wilkerson in favor of said Hays for the sum of (p 42) of one hundred and forty three dollars and twenty five Cents as given under our hands and seals this 19th Sept. 1812

                                            James Davis,   Seal

                                            Jere Brown,   Seal

Came to hand and levied the 21st Sept. 1812 on 341 acres of land on Suggs Creek as the property of Wyat Wilkerson a witness named. No other property found.

Thos. Bradley, S.W.C.

Which said attachment with the proceedings thereon were returned to Court at September Term 1812 and thereupon Came the said Harmon A. Hays by his attorney and made propert of the writing obligatory in the words and figures following.

On before the first day of May next I promise to pay or Cause to be paid unto Harmon A. Hays or order the just and full sum of one hundred & forty Dollars for value received of him as witness my hand & seal this 20th day April 1812.

Wyat Wilkerson, J. P.

Whereupon it appearing to the satisfaction of the Court that the defendant is not an inhabitant of this State.

It is ordered by the Court that all further proceedings in the above suit be stayed nine months agreeable to Act of Assembly.

(Continued)

(p 43) And now at the June term 1813 Came the plaintiff by his attorney Harry L. Douglass - And the Defendant Wyat Wilkerson, altho solemnly Called Came not nor is defence made, It is there fore Considered by the Court that the said Harmon A. Hays, recover of the said Defendant Wyat Wilkerson, his debt of one hundred and forty Dollars together with nine Dollars and ten cents damages and also his Cost by him about his suit in this behalf expended and that the land levied on be sold to satisfy said debt Damages and Costs.

And there upon an Execution or order of sale issued in the following words & figures (to wit)

State of Tennessee)
Wilson County Court)   To the Sheriff of said County.
                        Greeting.

You are hereby Commanded to expose to public sale three hundred & forty one acres of land the property of Wyat Wilkerson lying on Suggs Creek, adjoining Logues land begining at two dogwoods thence East 400 poles to a stake thence North 180 poles to a stake, thence West 225 poles to a stake thence South 100 poles to a stake, West 177 poles to a stake.

South 80 poles to the begining and thereby Cause to be made the sum of one hundred & forty nine dollars and ten Cents which lately in our Court (p 44) our Court of pleas and quarter sessions at June term 1813 Harmon A. Hays, recovered against said Wyatt Wilkerson by an original attachment for his debt and damages - also the sum of six Dollars forty seven Cents Costs of suit in that behalf expended where of the said Wyat Wilkerson is connected and liable to pay and the land levied on by said Attachment Condemned by the Court for the payment of said debt & damages as appears to us of record — and have you those money before the Justices of an ensuing Court of pleas and quarter sessions to be held at the Court house in the town of Lebanon on the third Monday in December next, then and there ready to render to the said Harmon A. Hays for his debt and Cost aforesaid — Herein paid not witness John Allcorn Clerk of our said Court at office this 3rd Monday in September 1813, and the 38th year of Am. Independence.

Jno. Allcorn, Clk.

Bill of Cost.

Attachment & law tax	$ 3.75
Laying attachment 100 1 continuance 40	1.40
Judgement & record 100 1 Execution 40	1.40
Attorney Douglass	2.50
	$66.75

Sold within named land
Dec. 4, 1813 to Harmon A. Hays for twelve Dollars.

W. Woodward, J. S.

(p 45) At a Court of pleas and quarter sessions began and held for the County of Wilson at Lebanon on Monday the 20th of June 1814 and of the Independence of the United States the 38th.

Present George Michie, Hugh Roam, Richard C. Craddock, Ransom Gwyn, & Marriot Davis Esq. who took their seats & proceeded to business &c.

SHADRACK GRIGG Plft.)
vs) Appeal Contd. on affidavit of Deft.
JOHN M. GREGORY Deft.)

GEORGE DONNELL Lessee Plft.)
vs) In Ejectment Contd. till next court.
JAMES SCOTT, Defendant)

J. & J. ALEXANDER Plft.)
vs) Certiorari
EDITH CAMPBELL, Deft.)

On Motion of the Defendants Counsel the proceedings in this Case to be quashed.

It is considered by the Court that the same be quashed on said motion and that the Defendant recover against the said Plaintiff all Costs that have accured on the same and that the Plft. go hence &c.

JOHN CARTWRIGT Plft.)
vs) Appeal
JOHN TELFORD Deft.)

By Consent this suit is Compromised & each party agree to pay an equal part of the Costs. It is there fore &c.

THOMAS DONNELL, Plft.)
vs) Certiorari
JUDIAH WILIE Deft.)

The referees appointed by order of last Court made and returned an award in the words and figures following, State of Tennessee Wilson County we the underneath Subsre S. (p 46) Arbitrator in Conformity to an order of Court to us directed from the County Court of Wilson have this day met at Esqr. Samuel Cannons in order to settle a dispute depending in a matter of Controversing between Thomas Donnell and Judiah Wiley and after hearing the witnesses on both sides we do award and say that Thomas Donnell pay to the said Wiley thirteen Dollars and ninety two Cents – and that each party pay an equal part of all expenses that now is due an all the proceedings that are now depending in the Court of said County and pay to each other general receipts, and be finally Clear of all demands previous to this date.

Given under our hands &c April 9th 1814.

Walter Carruth, James Williams, John W. Payton, Samuel Cannon, (Arbitrators) &c. It is therefore the opinion of the Court that the award be Confirmed as the Judge of this Court and that the said Wiley recover against the said Donnell the sum of thirteen dollars ninety two cents as by the referrence made and returned and that each party pay an equal part of the Costs in this suit expended &c.

Hugh Wilie a witness 2 days
Jas. McAdow 4 days
John Donnell a witness 4 days.

HUMPHEY DONELSON Lessee Plft.
vs   In Ejct.
GEORGE SMITH Defendant

Recd. one dollar my fee Hugh Wilie.

Ordered that Court adjourn untill to-morrow morning 9 o'clock.

Tuesday Morning Court met according to adjournment Present Christopher Cooper, George Michie, Walter Carruth, Deveraux Wynne, James Richmond, James Williams & James Stuart, Esqs. & proceeded to business.

(p 47) Records of June term 1814

HUMPHRY DONELSON, Lessee Plft.
vs   In Ejectment
GEORGE SMITH Deft.

This day came the parties by their attornies also a Jury of good and lawful men (to wit) Ephriam Farr, Phillip Johnson, Isham Wynne, Benjamin Bowers, John Ross, John Jennings, Robert Jinnings, Jacob McDermit, William Word, John Cage, David Caldwell, & Aaron Anglin, who being elected tried and sworn the truth to speak upon the issue joined upon their oaths do say they find the defendant is not guilty of the tresspass and ejectment in Manner and form as the plaintiff in declaring hath alledged.

It is therefore Considered by the Court that the Defendant go hence without day and that he recover against the said Plaintiff his Costs of suit by him in this behalf expended &c.
from which Judgement the said plaintiff prays an appeal to the next Circuit Court to be holden for the County of Wilson on the first Monday in September next at the Court house in Lebanon and upon the said Plantiff filing his reasons and entering into bond as the law directs.

It is considered by the Court that an appeal as aforesaid be granted &c.

David Smith a witness for the plaintiff proved two days
             attendance and 72 miles & 4 ferriges $5.13
William Donelson for the same proved 2 days attendance
             100 miles & 4 ferriges $6.25 cts.

(48) AARON STUART Plft.)
    vs   ) Appeal
JOHN PRUITTE Deft.) ~~Certorari~~

   Pursuant to an order of reference made at last term of referres made and returned an award in the following words and figures.

   We a Committee nominated and appointed by Jesse Rhodes Esquire according to an order of Court to him directed to arbitrate an appeal Aaron Stuart, against John Pruitte do find as follows to wit viz that John Pruitte, pay to Aaron Stuart the amount of a Judgement rendered against him by Jesse Rhodes, esqr. with all Cost accured thereon Lawyers fees Court Charges Constables fees where by we find for Stuart the plainliff.

   Given under our hands this 23rd day of April 1814.

   Jonathan Ozment. Soleman Bunch, Thos. Richmond, John Baird, Jacob Sullivan, test Jesse Rhodes, J.P.

   It is the opinion of the Court that the award be confirmed as the Judgment of this Court.

JOHN PRUITTE Plft.)
    vs   ) Certiorari
AARON STUART Deft.)

   We the Committee of references appointed as above do find as follows in the Case of the Certiorari John Pruitt Plaintiff and Aaron Stuart Defendant viz that John Pruitt pay all Cost and loose his demand against said Stewart given under our hand this 23rd April 1814.

           Jonathan Ozment, Soleman Burnet, Thos. Richmond, John Baird, Jacob Sullivan, Test Jesse Rhodes. It is considered by the Court that the above award be confered as the Judgement of this court.

(p 49) WILLIAM DAVIS Guardian Plft.)
     vs   ) Trovers &c Conversion
JESSE HOLT Defendant   )

   This day Came the parties by their attornies also a jury of good and lawful men to wit William Walker, John Merritt, William Edings, John Roach, Henry Reiff, William Palmer, Hugh Telford, Richard Anderson, Wm Baird, Joel Swindle, John Barber, & Martin Hancock, who being elected tried and sworn the truth to speak upon the issue joined upon their oaths do say they find that the said Defendant did take into his possession the Negro Woman Polly & converted the aforesaid Negro to his own use as the plaintiff in declaring hath alledged and assess the plaintiffs damage to four hundred and fifty dollars.

   It is therefore Considered by the Court that the said Plaintiff recover against the said Defendant the sum of four hundred and fifty as by the Jury aforesaid in form aforesaid assessed Also his Cost of suit in that be-half expended & the Deft. in Mercy

Motion by Defendant for a new trial. Motion for new trial withdrawn &c.

Gideon Carr, a witness for the plaintiff proved two days
              attendance
John Lambut, a witness for Deft. 3 days
Frances Palmer, a witness for Deft. 3 days
Aaron Lambut, a witness de.   3 days
Jere Tucker, a witness for Plft. 3 days.

THOMAS MAYS Plft.   }
    vs   } In Debt.
WILLIAM SHEPHARD   }

Dismissed at Defents. Costs –
The plaintiff Came into Court and assumed all Cost, It is therefore
Considered by the Court that the plaintiff pay the Cost &c.

(p 50) RICHARD KING Adms. Plft. }
        vs   } In Debt.
     JOHN MARSHALL Deft. }

This day Came the parties by their attorneys also a jury of good and lawful men to wit.

Ephriam Farr, Phillip Johnson, Isham Wynne, Benjamin Bonner, John Ross, Jacob Jennings, Robert Jinnings, Jacob McDermet, William Word, John Cage, David Caldwell, & Aaron Anglin, who being elected tried & sworn the truth to speak upon the issue joined upon their oaths do say they find the debt in the plaintiffs declaration mentioned amounting to one hundred and fourteen dollars twenty six Cents including Damages by interest.

It is therefore Considered by the Court that the said Plaintiff recover against the said Defendant the said sum of one hundred and fourteen dollars and twenty six Cents as by the Jury aforesaid in form aforesaid assessed also his costs of suit in that behalf expended.

THOMAS WILLIAMSON Plft. }
    vs   } Debt.
ADAM VINEYARD Deft. }

This day Came the Defendant by his attorney and the Plaintiff the solemnly called came not nor is his suit further prosecuted. It is therefore Considered by the Court that the Defendant go hence without day and he recover against the Plaintiff his Costs about his suit in that behalf expended &c.

(p 51) JOHN DEN Lessee of PHILLIP SHCKLER }
         vs   } In Ejectment
     JOHN BARBEE Deft. }

This day Came the parties by their attornies also a Jury of good and lawful men to wit Ephriam Farr, Phillip Johnson, Isham Wynne, Benjamine Bonner,

John Ross, Jacob Jennings, Robert Jinnings, Jacob McDermit, William Word, John Cage, David Caldwell, and Aaron Anglin, who being elected tried & sworn the truth to speak upon the issue joined upon their oaths do say, they find that the Defendant is guilty of the trespass & Ejectment as the plaintiff in declaring against him hath alledged and assess the plaintiffs damage to one Cent -

It is there-fore Considered by the Court that the Plaintiff recover ~~again~~ his term yet to ~~of~~ ~~and~~ ~~the~~ Came of and in the premises with the appurtenances, also his ~~costs~~ damages as by the jury aforesaid assessed also his Costs of suit in that behalf expended and that he have his writ of possession &c.

Wm. W. PORTERFIELD Lessee Plft.)
       vs   )   In Ejectment
HUGH BONE Deft.   )

This day Came the parties by their attornies also a jury of good and lawful man (to wit) Lewis Chambers, Benjamin Bonner, Phillip Johnson, Isham Wynne, John Ross, Ephraim Farr, Joshua Kelly, Edward Jacobs, Samuel Cheatham, Gideon Carr, Aaron Lambut, & William Davis, who being elected tried and sworn the truth to speak upon the issue joined upon their oaths do say they find the defendant is not gulity of the trespass & ejectment as the plaintiff in declaring hath alledged It is there fore considered by the Court that they defendt. go hence & recover against the Plaintiff his Cost &c.

(p 52) PORTERFIELD Lessee Plft.)
        vs   )
    HUGH BONE   Deft.   )

    John Scott, a witness for Defendant proved 3 days atten.
    Able Wason, a witness for Defendant 3 days atten.
    James Williams for Plft. 1 day
    Jno. Doak for Deft. 2 days.

MARY PATTON Plft.   )
     vs   )   Appeal
MURRIAT DAVIS Deft.)

On the Motion of the Defendants attorney It is Considered by the Court that this Cause be quashed and that the plaintiff pay all Costs below and that Deft. pay his own Witnesses &c.

GREGERY JOHNSON, Plft.)
     vs   )   Appeal
WILLIAM WALKER, Deft.)

Continued on affidavit of W. Walker.

JOHN HARPOLE Plft.)
      vs   )   In Debt.
TRUMAN MOGLIN Deft.)

       The Defendant in proper person Came into Court and acknowledges the same of a writ this day issued Waves all errors and informalities and Confesses the plaintiffs debt of three hundred and six dollars & fifty five Cents with twenty four dollars fifty two Cents Interest, Amounting in the whole to $331.07 cts.

       It is therefore Considered by the Court that the said Plaintiff recover against the Deft. the said sum of $331.07 cents as by the Deft. Confessed also Cost of this Judgement.

       18th August 1814 Recieved the full amount of the above judgement & cost

                                  John Harpole,
(p 53)   From the Appearance Docket.

SHADRACK GRIGG Plft.)
      vs   )   Appeal Contd.
JOHN W. GREGORY Deft.)

       This 20th day of September 1812 Came the parties by their attornies also a jury of good and lawful men to wit John Simpson, John A. Givens, William Wilson, Leonard Caplinger, George Donnell, Dudley Brown, Lewis Sheppard, Joseph Cole, Samuel Anderson, Robert Donnelson, Gilbreath Neel, & John Hubbard, who being elected tried and sworn the truth to speak upon the issue joined upon their oaths do say they find for the Plaintiff the sum of ten Dollars for his debt &c.

       It is therefore considered by the Court that the said Plaintiff recover against said Defendant the said sum of ten Dollars for his debt as by the jury aforesaid assessed also his Cost of suit in that behalf expended and that he have his Execution &c.   No. 1

       Anthony Seal, a witness proved thirteen Days as a Witness.
       Charles Haskins, a witness proved 4 days.
       George Clark, a witness 11 day attendance.

GEO. DONNELL, Plft.)
      vs   )   In Ejectment
JAMES SCOTT, Deft.)

       Condt. on affidavit of Plft. John Donelson forfeits as a witness according to act of assembly.

       Fredrick Davis proved 2 days 76 miles.

(p 54) JACOB HAMBLE   Plft.)
    vs   )   Indic.
 BEVERLY WILLIAMS & Others)   Atta.

  This day Came the plaintiff by his attorney and the Defendants being solemnly Called and Came not nor is any defence made. It is there fore Considered by the Court that the plaintiff recover Judgement according to specialty with Interest thereon.

  The plaintiffs attorney agree Execution be stayed untill next Court. No. 2.

JAMES WINCHESTER & CO. Plft.)
    vs   )   Case
OBEDIAH SPRADLEN, Adm. Deft.)

  Plead and try at next Court.   No. 3.

JOHN STUART Plft.)
    vs   )   Atta Plead & Try next Court. No. 4.
JOSHUA KELLY Deft.)

JOHN GALLAWAY Plft.)
    vs   )   Debt.
ABNER WASON   Deft.)

  Plead in abutment or plead and by the next term.   No. 5.

BENJAMIN HOOKER   Plft.)
    vs   )   In Covenant.   No. 6.
JOSEPH COLE   Deft.)

  Dismissed by the Plaintiff and Deft. assumes Costs.

(p 55) MATHEW SCOBY Plft.   )
    vs   )   In Debt.
 JOSEPH STUART & BLAKE RUTLAND Deft.)

  The Defendant Joseph Stuart Cames into Court and Confesses the plaintiffs debt amounting to $258.75 Interest amounting to two Dollars and fifteen Cents. Amounting to two hundred and sixty Dollars and ninety Cents -

  It is there fore Considered by the Court that the plaintiff recover against the said Defts. the said sum of two hundred and sixty dollars and ninety Cents for his debt and damage by way of Interest also his Cost of suit in that behalf expended. No. 7

JOEL MANN   Plft.)
    vs   )   Case Plead & try. No. 8
CLACK STONE Deft.)

JACOB NEIL)
    vs   )   No. 9
LAWRENCE SYPERT)

JESSE HOLT   Plft.)
    vs   )   Case plead & try next term.   No. 10
WILLIAM DAVIS Deft.)

CLACK STONE Plft.)
    vs   )   In Debt - Pleas to issue   No. 11
WILLIAM MANN, Deft.)

SAMUEL W. SHERRELL Plft.)
        vs   )   In Debt.
HULDA SHERRILL & Others, Defts.)

        Dismissed. No. 12.

(p 56)
SAMUEL ELLIOTT, Plft.)
       vs   )   In Debt.
STEPHENSON & RHODES Deft.)

     This day Came the Defendants in proper person and Confessed Judgement for the sum of one hundred and eighty five dollars Debt and five Dollars Interest.

     It is therefore Considered by the Court that the said Plaintiff recover against said Defendants the sum of one hundred and ninety Dollars as by said Defendant Confessed also his Costs of suit &c.   No. 13

BENJAMIN JOSLIN Plft.)
    vs   )   In Debt.
JOEL MANN & CLARK STONE Defts.)

     Plead and try next Court.   No. 14.

JOHN DEW Lessee of)
 JAMES WHITSET Plft.)
    vs   )   In Eject.
CHARLES HAYS Deft.)

     The Defendant enters into the Common rule and agrees on the trial of the Cause to Confess lease entry and Auster and rely on the tittle only, and Pleads not guilty & issue. No. 15

WILLIAM ADAMS Plft.)
     vs   )   Motion.
WILLIAM ENGLISH Deft.)

        On the motion of the Plaintiff by his Attorney It is Considered by
the Court it is Considered by the Court that the (p 57) two tracks of land
be Condemned and sold for the benefit of the Plfts. Judgement see the same
intered in full on the Minutes of Court at June T. 1814.   No. 16

GEO. A. ALLIN, Plft.   )
     vs   )   Case.
ROWLAND W. GRISSUM Deft.)

        Plead and try at next term.

(p 58) At a Court of pleas and quarter sessions began and held at the Court house in the town of Lebanon on the 19th day of September 1814 and 39th year of American Independence.

Present the worshipful George Michie, Joseph T. Williams, James Williams and Isaac Winston, esquires who took their seats and proceeded to business &c.

SHADRACK GRIGG   Plft. }
       vs   } Appeal.
JOHN W. GREGORY Deft. }

On this 20th of September 1814 Came the parties by their attornies also a jury of good and lawful men to wit John Simpson, John A. Givans, William Wilson, Leonard Caplinger, George Donnell, Dudley Brown, Lewis Sheppard, Joseph Cole, Samuel Anderson, Robert Donelson, Gilbreath Neil, John Hubbard, who being elected tried and sworn the truth to speak upon the issue joined upon their oaths do say they find for the Plaintiff the sum of ten Dollars for his Debt. It is therefore Considered by the Court that the said Plaintiff recover against the Defendant the sum of ten dollars as by the jury aforesaid assessed also his Cost of suit in that behalf expended.

GOERGE DONNELL   Plft. }
       vs   } In Ejectment
JAMES SCOTT   Deft. }

Continued on affidavit of the Plft. Frederick Davis a witness proved 2 days 76 miles.

(p 59) GREGORY JOHNSON Plft. }
           vs   } Appeal
        WILLIAM WALKER   Deft. }

This day Came the parties by their attornies also ~~I find of good and~~ ~~lawful men to wit~~ Also a jury of good and lawful men to wit John Simpson, John A. Givens, Leonard Caplinger, Dudley Brown, James Scoby, Charles Wade, Ship A. Puckett, William Jimmings, Samuel Brown, Robert Marshall, Jonathan Oxement, and John Taylor, who being elected tried and sworn the truth to speak upon the issue joined upon their oaths do say they find for the plaintiff the sum of nine Dollars for his debt.

It is therefore Considered by the Court that the said plaintiff recover against said defendant the said sum of nine Dollars as by the jury aforesaid assessed. Also his Cost of suit in that be-half expended &c from which Judgement the plaintiff prays an appeal to the next Circuit Court to be held for the County of Wilson in Lebanon on the first Monday in March next and upon his filing reasons and entering into bond with Charles Bennett & Edwd Crutcher his securities the appeal is granted &c.

JAMES WINCHESTER   Plft. }
       vs   } Case
OBEDIAH SPRADLIN   Deft. }

(p 60) JOHN STUART   Plft.)
)   Case
        vs   )
        JOSHUA KELLY   Deft.)   Judicial Atta.

JOHN GALLAWAY   Plft.)
)   In Debt.
        vs   )
ABNER WASSON   Deft.   )

    Dismissed on Defendants assuming the Costs. It is therefore considered by the Court that the said Plaintiff recover against the Defendant his Cost of suit in this behalf expended &c.

JOEL MANN   Plft.)
)   In Case
        vs   )
CLACK STONE Deft.   )

    Depositions taken by Consent by both parties on a Notice of 20 days Decleration filed time to plead so as not to delay trial.

JACOB NEIL   Plft.)
)   Case
        vs   )
LAWRENCE SYPERT   Deft.)

    Judgement of non prof.

JESSE HOLT   Plft.)
)   Case
        vs   )   Cont'd.
WILLIAM DAVIS   Deft.   )

    Guardian.

(p 61) BENJAMIN JOSLIN   Plft.)
)   Debt
        vs   )   Contd.
        JOEL MANN & CLACK STONE   Deft.)

JOHN DEN Lessee of
JAMES WHITSET   Plft.)
)   In Eject.
        vs   )   Contd.
CHARLES HAYES   Deft.   )

GEO. A. ALLIN   Plft.)
)   Case Dismissed.
        vs   )
ROWLAND W. GRISSUM Deft.)

    each party to pay half Costs.

PATRICK DARBY   Plft.)
)   Appeal.
        vs   )
DOUGLASS C. PUCKET   Deft.)

The Plaintiff being called and not appearing nor is his suit further prosecuted, on Motion of the Defendant by Harry L. Douglass his attorney it is Considered by the Court that the Defendant go hence without day and that he recover against said Plaintiff his Cost of suit in that behalf expended.

WILLIAM ANDERSON Plft. }
    vs   } Appeal the Plaintiff.
RICHARD ANDERSON Deft. }

       Non prop'd.

WILLIAM FRENCH Plft. }
    vs   } Appeal Contd.
ANDREW SOMERS Deft. }

(p 62) Pleas before the court of pleas and quarter sessions held for the County Wilson at the Court house in Lebanon on Monday the 19th day of December 1814 39th Year of Am. Independence.

Present Joseph T. Williams, William Robb, and Walter Caruth, Justices who took their seats and proceeded to business.

DONNELL Lessee Plft.)
vs.) In Eject.
JAMES SCOTT Deft.)

Contd. on the Affidavit of the Plaintiff Frederick Davis a witness proved one days attendance and 76 miles traveling.

JAMES WINCHESTER Plft.)
vs) Debt.
OBEDIAH SPRADLIN Deft.)

JOHN STUART Plft.)
vs) Case
JOSHUA KELLY Deft.)

On this 24th day of December 1814 Came the parties by their attornies also a jury of good and lawful men (to wit) Thomas Walson, Henry Brown, Patrick Anderson, Lewis Shepperd, Rowland Sutton, John Cage, Lard Sellars, Henry Palmer, John Presley, Freeman Modglin, William Babb, and Jesse Lock, who being elected tried and sworn the truth to speak upon the issue joined upon their oaths do say they find the Defendant did assume upon himself in manner and form as the plaintiff (p 63) in his declaration hath alledged and assess the Plaintiffs damages to one hundred & 20 dollars.

It is therefore Considered by the Court that the said Plaintiff recover against the said Defendant the sum of one hundred and twenty dollars as by the jury aforesaid assessed also his Cost of suit in that behalf expended & the Defendant &c.

John Bonner a witness for Plft. proved 5 days.
Jones Lock, a witness for def. proved 5 days.

JOEL MANN Plft.)
vs) Case
CLACK STONE Deft.)

Refered to arbitrators to be Chosen by the parties who's award is to be the Judgement of this Court.

JESSE HOLT Plft.)
vs) Case Contd.
WILLIAM DAVIS, Deft.)

BENJAMIN JOSLIN   Plft.   )
      vs   )   Debt.
CLACK STONE & Others Deft.)

       Declaration filed.

JOHN DEN   Lessee   )
      vs   )   In Ejectment.
CHARLES HAYS   Deft.   )

       Transfered to the Circuit Court by Consent.

WILLIAM FRENCH   **Plft.**)
      vs   )   Appeal Contd. by Consent.
ARDEN SOMERS   Deft.)

CORNELIUS JOINER, PLFT.   )
      vs   )   Case Contd.
RICHARD MARLOW, Deft.   )

(p 64) Justices present Jo T. Williams, John Harmat & Jos. McAdow.

CLACK STONE, Plft.   )
      vs   )   In Debt.
WILLIAM MANN Deft   )

      On this 22nd day of Dec. 1814 Came the parties by their attorney also a jury of good and lawful men to wit Peter Mosley, Jesse Hunt, William Howard, John Scoby, John Young, John Phillips, Richard Ramsey, Carter Irby, John Rea, John Davis, Alexander Carruth & Richard Phelps, who being elected tried and sworn the truth to speak upon the issue joined upon their oaths do say they find the Defendant hath not paid the Debt in the Plaintiffs declaration mentioned amounting to one hundred and seventy five dollars and assess the Plaintiffs damages occasioned by the detention of said debt to ten dollars & fifty Cents amounting in the whole to one hundred and eighty five dollars and fifty Cents. It is there fore Considered by the Court that the said Plaintiff recover against the said Defendant the sum of one hundred and eighty five dollars & fifty Cents the debt and damages as by the jury aforesaid in form aforesaid assessed also his Cost of suit in that be half expended & the Deft. in Mercy &c.

JUSTICE RULEMAN   Plft.   )
      vs   ) Tresspass, assault & battery.
WILL PIGG, JAS. CUNNINGHAM, & CORDER Deft.)

      This day Came the plft. by his Attorney and James Cunningham one of the Defendants by his Attorney also a jury of good and lawful men (to wit) (p 65) Peter Mosely, Jesse Hunt, William Howard, John Scoby, John Young, John Phillips, Richard Ramsey, Carter Irby, John Rea, John Davis, Alexander Caruth, & Richard Phelps, who being elected tried and sworn the truth to speak upon the issue joined upon their oaths do say they find the Defendant guilty of the trespass assault and battery as the Plaintiff against him hath Complained and assess the Plaintiffs damages to ten dollars.

It is therefore Considered by the Court that the plaintiff recover against the Defendant the said sum of ten dollars as by the Jury aforesaid in form aforesaid assessed also his Costs of suit in that behalf expended &c.

50¢ paid J. Standefer
Sally Hooks, a witness proved one days attendance.
Mary Renshaw, witness proved three days attendance pd.
Matilda Renshaw do   do   three days   do   pd.
Holliway Kee   do   do   three days   do   pd.
William Massee   do   for Deft. three days do   pd.
John Standefer   do   for three days   do

ISAAC PIERCE   Plft.)
      vs   ) Certiorari Contd.
I. & E. LINSEY Deft.)

Ordered that Court adjourn untill Court in Course.

John Bonner,   )
Joseph Johnson,)
Edmund Crutcher,)

(p 66) At a Court of Pleas and quarter sessions began and held for the County of Wilson at the Court house in Lebanon on the 20th day of March 1815 & 39th Year of American Independence.

Present the worshipful Christhoper Cooper, George Michie, and James Hinderson, Esquirs who took their seals & proceeded to business.

GEORGE DONNELL, Lessee Plft.
     vs — Ejectment
JAMES SCOTT, Defendant

This day Came the parties by their attorneys & thereupon a jury of good & lawful men to wit William H. Peace, William McKnight, John Cartwright, John Simpson, Notly Maddox, Robert Brown, William Foster, James Turner, Jesse Bloodworth, Simpson Organ, & John Foster, who being elected tried & sworn the truth to speak to speak upon the issue joined by Consent of the party & with the assent of the Court John Foster, one of the Jurors aforesaid is with drawn & the rest discharge from rendering their verdict therin.

JAMES WINCHESTER & CO. Plft.
     vs — Case
OBEDIAH SPRADLIN Deft.

Demurred overruled and a responded auster awarded.

JOEL MANN Plft.
     vs — Case
CLACK STONE Deft.

Rule of last Court extended.

(p 67) JESSE HOLT Plft.
     vs — Case Contd.
Wm. DAVIS Adm. Deft.

Plft. in Army.

BENJAMIN JOSLIN Plft.
     vs — Debt Contd.
CLACK STONE & Others Deft.

JOHN BEN Lessee of
JAS WHITESIDE Plft.
     vs — Eject. Contind.
CHARLES HAYS Deft.

WILLIAM FRENCH Plft.
     vs — Appeal Contd. on affidavit of Deft.
ARDEN SOMERS Deft.

CORNELIUS JONES, Plft.)
vs   ) Case Contd. Deft. In Army.
RICHARD MARLOW   Deft.)

JUSTICE RULEMAN, Plft.)
vs   ) T. A. Battery 22nd March 1815.
SHADRACK CORDER, Deft.)

This day Came the parties by their attorniey also a jury of good and lawful men to wit John Cartwright, Jesse Bloodworth, Alexander Astin, Everett Mitchell, Jeremiah Tucker, John Simpson, Joshua Bradberry, William New, Scott Riggs, Charles Locke, William H. Peace, and James Hunter who being elected tried and sworn the truth to speak upon the issue joined upon their oaths do say they find the Defendant guilty of the tresspass assault and battery Committed on the body of the plaintiff as he in his declaration hath alledged and assess (p 68) the damages done the plaintiff to ten dollars. It is therefore Considered by the Court that the said plaintiff recover of the said defendant the said sum of Ten Dollars the Damages aforesaid by the jury aforesaid assessed also his Costs of suit in that behalf expended and the Deft. &c.

Mary Renshaw, a witness for the plft. 4 days.
Matilda Renshaw, witness for the plft. 4 days.
Wm. Massy, a witness for Deft. proved 4 days 24 miles.
John Standefer   "   "   "   "   4 days.
James Cunningham "   "   "   "
Holloway Key,   "   "   "   "

ISAAC PIERCE   Plft.)
vs   ) Certiorari Continued on the
J. & E. LINSEY Deft.) affidavit of E. Linsey.

WILLIE BLOUNT, Governor Plft.   )
vs   ) Debt.
Wm. PITMAN, // ////// // // ////// Deft.)

//// //// //// ///////////// // //////

This day Came the parties by their Attornies also a jury of good and lawful men to wit Jonas Bradley, William Babb, Duke Wortham, James Edwards, John Coe, Peter Moore, Henry Chandler, John Harpole, Nathaniel Davis, William Thompson, William McKnight & Isham Wynne, who being elected tried and sworn the truth to speak upon the issue joined (p 69) upon their oaths do say they find the Defts. hath paid part of the debt in the Plfts. decleration mentioned but that there remains unpaid the sum of thirteen dollars and eighty seven Cents which they find for the said Plaintiff, It is therefore Considered by the Court that the said plaintiff recover against the said Defendants the sum of thirteen dollars eighty seven Cents as by the jury aforesaid assessed.

Also his Costs of suit in that behalf expended.

Afterwards to wit the same day Came the Plaintiff by his attorney and acknowledges to have recd. full satisfaction from the said Defendants for the amount of the aforesaid Judgement.

The Defendant assumes the Cost of suit.

WILLIE BLOUNT, Governor Plft.   )
       vs   )   Debt.
ROGER QUARLS, & L. H. LEWIS Deft.)

This suit is Consolidated with the above.

BENJAMIN MOTLEY Plft.   )
       vs   )   Case Continued on affidavit of the Plft.
BANISTER ANDERSON Deft.)

JOHN DEN Lessee D. BILLINGS Plft.)
          vs   )   Eject.
JOSEPH WILEY Deft.   )

This day Came the parties by their attornies & (p 70) and thereupon Came a jury of good and lawful men to wit John Cartwright, Jesse Bloodworth, William H. Peace, William McKnight, Everett Mitchell, John Simpson, William Crawford, Seth P. Pool, Thomas Harrington, Simpson Organ, William New, and David Rice, who being elected tried & sworn the truth to speak upon the issue joined returned from the bar to consult of their verdict but could not agree.

Whereupon by Consent of the parties and with the assent of the Court David Rice one of the Jurors aforesaid and is with drawn and the rest of the jurors discharged from rendering a verdict thereon.

Patrick McEakern, a witness for the Plaintiff proved 3 days at 100 cts. per day and 28 miles traveling.

JAMES CRYER Plft.   )
     vs   )   Debt.
JOHN B. PARKER Deft.)

This day Came the parties by their attornies, also a jury of good and lawful men to wit James H. Hunter, William Babb, Charles Lock, Henry Chandler, John Coe, Jesse Bloodworth, John Cartwright, William McKnight, Isham Wynne, John Harpole, John Simpson, and Richard Anderson, who being elected tried and sworn the truth to speak upon the issue joined, upon their oaths do say they find the defendant hath not paid the debt in the Plft. declaration mentioned and find for the plft. a balance of his debt amounting to one hundred and sixty three dollars and (p 71) and twenty one Cents, and assess the plaintiff damages occasioned by the detention of said balance of debt to five dollars and twelve Cents. It is therefore considered by the Court that the said Plaintiff recover against said Defendant the sum of one hundred and sixty three dollars twenty one Cents for the balance of his debt also five dollars twelve Cents for his damages as by the jury aforesaid assessed amounting in

the whole to one hundred sixty eight dollars and twenty three Cents, Also
his Cost of suit &c. the Defendant in Mercy &c.

WILLIAM BLOODWORTH & Others Plft.)
     Lessee of &c.)
        vs)   Eject.
JAMES CRAWFORD Deft.)

    Continued on affidavit.

    John Donelson a witness proved 4 days 40 miles.
    John Rice, a witness proved 4 days.
    David Rice " " " 4 days.

    Appearance Docket at March Term 1815.

THOMAS KEIFF, Plft.)   22nd March 1815
    vs)   Debt.
WILLIS DILLARD Deft.)

    The Defendant in his own person Comes into Court and acknowledges
the plfts. debt amounting to one hundred eighty seven dollars & fifty Cents
and two Dollars forty seven and a half Cents interest thereon. It is therefore Considered by the Court that the Plft. recover against the Deft. the
sum of one hundred & Eighty seven dollars and fifty Cents for his debt.
Two Dollars forty seven & a half Cents Interest. Also his Cost of suit &c.

(p 73) Pleas before the Court of pleas and quarter sessions began and held for the County of Wilson at the Court house in the town of Lebanon the 19th day of June 1815 and thirty ninth year of Am. Independence.

Justices present,
William Steele, Christopher Cooper, James Williams, and Marriat Davis, Esqs. who took their seats and proceeded to business,

A grand jury drawn from the original venire to wit John K. Wynne, foreman Jeremiah Tucker, John Green, Joseph Kirkpatrick, John G. Graves, Robert Edwards, Thomas Hern, James Welch, Hugh Telford, Samuel Brown, Thomas Wooldridge, Charles Cox, & Edward Moore, who being empanneled sworn Charged and sent to enquire for the body of the County &c.

GEORGE DONNELL Lessee Plft.)
              vs   ) In Ejectment.
JAMES SCOTT Deft.)

This day Came the parties by their attornies also a jury of good and lawful men to wit - Joseph Cole, Samuel Stuart, Lard Sellars, John Johnson, Allen Ratley, Thomas Carver, Milberry Hern, Sterling Tarpley, William Wilson, James Wiley, Martin Hancock and John Horn, who being elected tried and sworn the truth to speak upon the issue joined upon their oaths do say the Defendand is guilty of the tresspass and ejectment in manner and form as the plaintiff in declariring against him hath alledged and assess the plaintiffs damage to one Cent. It is therefore Considered by the Court that the said Plaintiff recover against (p 74) against the said Defendant his term yet to Come of & in the premises and appurtenances aforesaid together with the damages aforesaid by the jury aforesaid assessed.

Also his Cost by him about his suit in this behalf expended and that he have his writ of possession &c.

John Donelson, a witness for the Plaintiff proved four days attendance and 40 miles traveling.

JAMES WINCHESTER &C Plft.)
              vs   ) In Case.
OBEDIAH SPRADLIN Admr. Deft.)

Issue to the first plea and Demurrer to the next - Cont'd.

JOEL MANN, Plft.)
        vs   ) In Case.
GLACK STONE Deft.)

Rule of Reference intended.

JESSE HOLT, Plft.)
        vs   ) In Case.
WILLIAM DAVIS Deft.)

This day Came the parties by their attornies also a jury of good and lawful min (to wit) Dennis Kelly, Ryland Chandler, William Draper, John M.

Simpkins, Aaron Lambut, Seth P. Pool, Warner Lambeth, Samuel Cartwright, Edmund Turner, John Stone, Josiah Jones, & William Babb, (p 75) who being elected tried and sworn the truth to speak upon the issue joined upon their oaths do say they find the Defendant is not guilty in Manner and form as the plaintiff against him hath alledged. It is therefore Considered by the Court that the Defendant go hence without day and recover against the said plaintiff his Costs of suit in this behalf expended &c.

BENJAMIN JOSLIN   Plft.   )
            vs   )   In Debt.
CLACK STONE   & Others Deft.)

        This cause adjourned to the Circuit Court by Consent.

                                        June 21, 1815,

JOHN DEN Lessee J. WHITSET, Plft.)
            vs   )   In Eject.
CHARLES HAYS, Deft.   )

        This day Came the parties by their attornies also a jury of good and lawful min to wit Joseph Cole, Samuel Stuart, Lard Sellars, John Johnson, William Draper, Thomas Carver, Milberry Hern, Sterling Tarpley, Martin Hancock, Isham Wynne, Joel Echols, & Ryland Chandler who being elected tried and sworn the truth to speak upon the issue joined upon their oaths do say they find that the defendant is guilty of the tresspass and Ejectment in Manner and form as the Plaintiff in declaring against him hath alledged and assess the plaintiff's damage to one Cent. It is therefore Considered by the Court that the plaintiff recover (p 76) against the said defendant his term yet to Come of and in the premises with the appurtinances aforesaid in form aforesaid assessed together with his Cost of suit in this behalf expended and that he have his writ of possession granted him &c.

WILLIAM FRENCH Plft.   )
            vs   )   Appeal
ARDEN SOMERS   Deft.   )

        The Defendant Comes into court and with draws his defence and Confesses Judgement for the amount of the Judgement by the Justice of the peace with interest up to this 20th June 1815.

        Amounting to seven Dollars ninety seven Cents.

        It is therefore Considered by the Court that the said Plaintiff recover against the said Defendant the said sum of seven Dollars 97 cents as by said Defendant Confesses also his Cost in this behalf expended.

CORNELIUS JOINER   Plft.)
        vs   )   Case on Motion.
RICHARD MARLOW   Deft.)

     Judgement by default set aside & Deft. Please not guilty & statute of limitation &c.

ISAAC PRICE   Plft.)
      vs   )   Certiorari
J. & E. LINSEY   Deft.)

     Executors of John Linsey dec'd. Motion to quash the proceedings of the Justice of the peace overruled by the Court and on this 21st day of June 1815 Came a jury of good and lawful men (to wit) Dennis Riley, Joseph Cole, Samuel Stuart (p 77) Lard Sellars, John Johnson, Wm. Draper, Thomas Carver, Ryland Chandler, Milbry Hern, Sterling Tarpley, Edward Turner, and Samuel Cartwright, who being elected tried and sworn to will and truly try the matter of Controversy between the parties aforesaid upon their oaths do say they find for the Plaintiff a balance of his debt amounting to fifteen dollars.

     It is therefore Considered by the Court that the said plaintiff recover against the said Defendant as executor of John Linsey, dec. the said sum of fifteen dollars.for his debt to be levid off the goods & Chattels rights & Credits of the deceased if to be found in the hands of the said Executor, also his Costs of suit in this behalf expended.

BENJAMIN MOTLEY   Plft.)
      vs   )   Case
BANISTER ANDERSON   Deft.)

     Be it remembered that here to fore (to wit) at December Term 1814 Banister Anderson was attached to answer Benjamin Motley of a plea of Tresspass on the Case to his Damage two hundred dollars.

     Whereupon at said Term the said Benjamin Motley, by Harry L. Douglass, his attorney filed his declaration in the following words & figures (to wit)

                             State of Tennessee)   December Term
                             Wilson County   )   1814

     Benjamin Motley by his attorney Complains of Banister Anderson, in Custody &c of a plea of trespass on the Case for that the said Banister (to wit) at the County of Wilson aforesaid inconsideration that the said Benjamin had sold to the said (p 78) said Banister a Certain bay horse of the value of eighty Dollars then and there undertook & faithfully promised to pay the said Motley the said sum of eighty dollars when he should be there to afterwards requested and whereas the said Banister on the day and year aforesaid at the County aforesaid in Consideration that the said

Benjamin had sold to the said Banister another horse of the value of eighty dollars, he the said Banister then and there undertook & faithfully promised to pay to the said Benjamin so much money as the said other horse was worth - and the said Benjamin avert the said horse was worth other the sum of eighty dollars. Yet the said Banister not regarding his said promises and undertakings but fraudulantly intending Craftily & subtely to deceive & defraud the said Benjamin and in this behalf hath not paid said sum of money or other of them but hath dishonestly refused hitherto to pay the same to the damage of the said Benjamine one hundred and fifty Dollars and therefore he sues.

                                                    Douglass Atto.

    At said December term 1814 the Defendant in this Case by his attorney William Hadley Esquire Comes and defends the wrong and injury where he and says that he did not undertake or promise in manner and form as the said Benjamin against him hath declared and of this he puts himself upon the County -

    And the plaintiff likewise.

                                        Wm. Hadly Atto.
                                        H. L. Douglass, for Plft.)

    And for further plea in this behalf the said Defendant saith that the said Benjamin his (p 79) his action aforesaid against him aught not to have or maintain because he saith that he at the time of Making the several promises set forth in the plaintiffs declaration was within the age of twenty one years and this he is ready to verify.-

    Wherefore he prays judgment the said Plaintiff his action aforesaid against him aught to have and Maintain

    Wm. Hadly atto. for the Deft. Demurrer & Joiner & /////.

                                        Douglass Atto. Plft.

/&// //// /// // //// ////

    At March Term 1815 Came the parties by their attornies and by Consent the following rule of Court is made (to wit) Cont'd as on affidavit of the plaintiff.

    At June Term 1815, Came the parties aforesaid by their attornies also a jury of good & lawful men to wit John K. Wynne, Robert Edwards, Samuel Stuart, William Draper, Joseph Cole, Thomas Sypart, John G. Graves, Hugh Telford, Samuel Brown, Edward Moore, Jeremiah Tucker, and William Melone, who being elected tried and sworn the truth to speak upon the issue joined upon their oaths do say they find the said Defendant ////// did assume upon him self in Manner and form as the plaintiff in declering against him hath alledged and assess the plaintiffs damage to eighty Dollars.

It is therefore Considered by the Court that the said plaintiff recover against the said Defendant the sum of Eighty dollars as by the Jurors aforesaid in form aforesaid assessed also his Costs in suit in this behalf expended and the Deft. in Mercy &c.

From which Judgement the Defendant prays an appeal to the next Circuit Court to be held for the County of Wilson on the first Monday in September next.

Upon his entering into bond as the law directs with T. Bradly & T. Wooldred security an appeal is granted him. And filing reasons. Copy record made out.

(p 80) WILLIAM BLOODWORTH Lessee Plft.)
               vs   )   In Ejectment
       JAMES CRAWFORD   Deft.   )

Contd. as on affidavit of the plaintiff.

William Nash witness for the plaintiff proved 3 days attendance and 34 miles.
       John Donelson, a witness 3 days and 40 miles.
       John Rice a witness 2 days
       David Rice, a witness 3 days.
       Robert Thompson a witness 3 days 72 miles.

                                                    22nd June

WILLIAM MOORE Plaintiff   )
               vs   )   Debt.
JO CASTLEMAN, JNO W. LUMPKIN Deft.)

This day Came the parties by their attorney also a jury of good and lawful men to wit, Dennis Kelly, Samuel Stuart, Lard Sellars, John Johnson, Thomas Carver, Ryland Chandler, Sterling Tarpley, James Welch, Charles Cox, Thomas Wooldridge, John Green, and Elijah Gross, who being elected tried and sworn the truth to speak upon the issue upon their oaths do say they find the said defendants hath not paid the debt in the debt in the plaintiffs delaration Mentioned amounting to one hundred and fifty five dollars, and assess the plaintiffs damages occasioned by the detention of said debt to five dollars and twenty Cents. It is there Considered by the Court that the said Plaintiff recover against the said defendants the said sum of one hundred and fifty five dollars for his debt also the sum of five dollars twenty five Cents for his damages as by the jury aforesaid assessed also his Costs of suit in this be-half expended & the Defts. in Mercy &c.

(p 81) JOHN HOWARD   Plft.   )
               vs   )   Case Refered at last term.
       FRANCIS SANDERS, Deft.   )

Robert Edwards, William Donnell, Robert Alexander, John Doak, and John Qusenberry chosen by the party) who made out and exhibited the following award to wit, John Howard, is to pay for the plank at the rate of sawing so much of plank as is Customary for sawing plank of the same discription and said Howard is to pay the Costs of summoning his witnesses & the aforesaid witness claiming their Attendance and said Francis Sanders is to pay his witnesses and the officer for summoning said witness and the said Howard is to dismiss the suit in Court. and pay all Cost in Court we also Consider that John Howard took the plank in error given under our hands this 1st day of April 1815 Robert Edwards, William Donnell, Robert Alexander, John Doak & John Quesenberry. It is therefore Considered by the Court that the above award be the Judgement of this Court and that the Defendant recover against the said Plaintiff his Costs in Court in this be-half expended, and the Plaintiffs suit Dismissed.

JOHN DEN, Lessee of Plft.)
JACOB LASITER   )   In Ejectment.
        vs   )
THOMAS STUART   Deft.   )

Continued on affidavit of Defendant and Considered by the Court that the Defendant pay the Cost of William Nashes, attendance as a witness at this term amounting to three dollars.

(p 82) WILLIE BLOUNT, Governor Plft.)
        vs   )   Cont.
BENJAMIN TARVER, & JACOB THOMAS Deft.)

Continued as on affidavit of Defendant.

JOHN DEN Lessee of   )
DAVID BILLINGS, Plaintiff.   )
        vs   )   Ejectment
JOSEPH WILEY, Defendant.   )

David Billings the Plaintiff in this action Comes into Court and refuses further to prosecute his suit. It is there fore Considered by the Court that his suit of ejectment be dismissed and that the Defendant recover against the said Plaintiff his Costs of suit in this behalf expended &c.

BLAKE RUTLAND Plft.   )
        vs   )   In Covenant.
JOHN H. LIGAN Deft.   )

This day Came the parties by their attornies also a jury of good and lawful men to wit Demis Kelly, Lard Sellars, John Johnson, Thomas Carver, Ryland Chandler, Milberry Hern, Sterling Tarpley, James Welch, Charles Cox, Thomas Wooldridge, John Green & Thomas Hern, who being elected tried and sworn the truth to speak upon the issue joined upon their oaths do say they find the Defendant hath not kept his Covenant, but hath broken the same to the damage of the plaintiff one hundred and sixteen dollars & three Cents.

It is Considered by the Court that the plaintiff recover against the Defendant the sum of one hundred & sixteen Dollars & three Cents for his damages as by the Jury aforesaid in form aforesaid assessed Also his Costs of suit in this behalf expended &c.

ALEXANDER KIRKPATRICK Plft. }
     vs   Covenant.
MARRIOTT DAVIS Deft. }

This day Came the parties by their attornies also a Jury of good and lawful men to wit Dennis Kelly, Lard Sellars, John Johnson, Thomas Carver, Ryland Chandler, Melberry Hern, Sterling Tarpley, James Welch, Charles Cox, Thomas Wooldridge, John Green, & Thomas Hern, who being elected tried and sworn the truth to speak upon the issue joined upon their oaths do say the Defendant did not assume upon him self in manner & form as the plaintiff against him hath performed his promise assumpsit.

It is there fore Considered ~~occasioned by the detention of the said debt to fifteen dollars & eighteen Cents. It is therefore Considered by the Court that the said Plaintiff recover against the defendant the debt & damages aforesaid as by the jurors aforesaid assessed &c Also his Costs of suit &c.~~

~~(b.84) Records of June Term 1815~~

~~WILLARD & WIFE Plft. }~~
~~vs~~ ~~Trespass~~
~~WYATT BETTIE Deft. }~~

~~Refered to Arbitrators.~~

~~This day Came the parties by their attornies also a jury of good and lawful men to wit Dennis Kelly, Samuel Stuart, Lard Sellars, John Johnson, Thomas Carver, Ryland Chandler, Sterling Tarpley, James Welch, Charles Cox, Thomas Wooldridge,~~ by the Court that the plaintiff take nothing by his bill and that the Defendant go hince without day and recover against the said plaintiff his Costs of suit in this behalf expended.

JOHN WATSON, Plft. }
     vs   In Debt.
EDMUND FLETCHER, Deft. }

This day Came the parties by their attornies also a jury of good and lawful men to wit, Dennis Kelly, Samuel Stuart, Lard Sellars, John Johnson, Thomas Carver, Ryland Chandler, Sterling Tarpley, James Welch, Charles Cox, Thomas Wooldridge, John Green, & Thomas Hern, who being elected tried & sworn the truth to speak upon the issue joined upon their oaths do say the Defendant hath not paid the debt in the plaintiffs decleration mentioned amounting to ninety seven dollars and ninety four Cents - and assess the Plaintiffs damage occasioned by the detention of the said debt to fifteen dollars & eighteen Cents. It is therefore Considered by the Court that the said plaintiff recover against the said defendant the debt & damages aforesaid as by the Jurors aforesaid assessed & also his cost of suit.

(p 84)

HILLARD & WIFE Plft)
       VS   ) Tresspass -- Refered to arbitrators
WYATT BETTIS Deft)

Lewis McCartney Plft. vs Joshua Kelly Deft. In Debt

      This day came the parties by their attornies also a jury of good and lawful men to wit Dennis Kelly, Samuel Stuart, Lard Sellars, John Johnson, Thomas Carver, Ryland Chandler, Sterling Tarpley, James Welch, Charles Cox, Thomas Wooldridge, John Green & Thomas Hern, who being elected tried and sworn the truth to speak upon the issue joined upon their oaths do say the defendant hath not paid the debt on the plaintiffs declaration mentioned of one hundred and twenty nine dollars an assess his damages occasioned by the detention of said debt to twenty dollars and five cents. It is therefore considered by the court that the plaintiff recover against the said defendant the the sum of one hundred and fifty five dollars & five cents the debt & damages as by the jury aforesaid in form aforesaid assessed also his costs of suit in that behalf expended.

CHRISTOPHER BULLARD Plft.)
       VS   ) Appeal
JO STACY SEN. & JO STACY JR. Deft)

      This day came the Plft. by his attorney and the appelants failing to appear within the time prescribed by law and prosecute their appeal whereupon motion of the plaintiffs attorney is consided by the court that the appeal be dismissed & that the judgement of the Justice of (p 85) the peace be affirmed and that the said plaintiff recover against the said defendants and F. Young their security the sum of thirty dollars as by the justice of the peace adjudged also his cost of suit in that behalf expended &.

JOEL MANN Plft.)
     VS   ) Appeal
SETH P. POOL Deft)

      This day came parties appellee by their attorney and thereupon a jury of good men therein appel towit failing to appear within the three two first days of the term and prosecute his appeal. It is therefore on motion of the appellee by his attorney considered by the court that the judgement of the magistrate be affirmed & that the said appellee recover of the said appellant & his securities William New, his debt of seventeen dollars and ninety two cents & also his cost by him about his suit in this behalf expended &

HARRY & JACOB COOK Plft)
       VS   ) Appeal
ISHAM DAVIS Deft)

      This day came the parties by their attornies also a jury of good and lawful men to wit, John K. Wynne, Robert Edwards, Samuel Stuart, Wm. Draper, Joseph Cole, Joseph Kirkpatrick, John G. Graves, Hugh Telford, Samuel Brown, Edward Moore, Jeremiah Tucker & Frances Anderson, who being elected tried and sworn the truth to speak on the matter of controversy in said suit now on trial upon their oaths do say they find for the (p 86) for the appalant the sum of eleven dollars due on his account, It is therefore considered by the court that the said appalant recover against the appalee the said sum of eleven dollars also his costs of suit in that behalf expended &.

William Goodall a witness for the appalant proved two days and 40 miles traveling & two ferriges amounting to three dollars seventy two & a half cents $3.72½ cents.

JORDAN WORD Appalant)
     VS   ) Appl.
JEREMIAH TAYLOR Appalee)

       This day came the appalanthy his attorney and the appalee failing to appear within the two first days of the term and prosecute his appeal It is therefore considered by the court that the judgement of the Justice of the peace be reversed ~~for fourteen dollars twelve and half cents~~ and that the appalee recover his cost of suit his the appalee & James Ewing his security &&.

MICHAEL WILSON Plft.)
     VS   ) Appl.
ALLEN RACKLY Deft)

       This day came the parties by their attornies also a jury of good and lawful men (to wit) Dennis Kelly, Lard Sellars, John Johnson, Thomas Carver, Ryland Chandler Milberry Hern, Sterling Tarpley, James Welch, Charles Cox, Thomas Wooldridge, John Green, and Thomas Hern who being elected tried and sworn the truth to speak on the matter in dispute (p 87) upon their oaths do say the find for the defendant It is therefore considered by the court that that the defendant go hence without day and that he recover against the appalant his cost of suit in this behalf &&.

Nancy Ashford a witness proved 4 days
John Hollinsworth do   do 4 days
James Byrns   do   do 4 days
John Walker   do   do 4 days

       From the appearance Docket June Term 1815

ROSS WEBB Plaintiff)
     VS   ) Certiorari
JOHN B. GOFNEY Deft)
       Death of Webb suggested -

       It is agreed by the parties that the cause shall be tried on the motion to dismiss and the merrit also if necessary at the next term
                        Foster & Doug. Attoy.

MATTHEW FIGURES Plft.)
     VS   ) 22nd June 1815
WILLIAM C. TUCKER Deft.) Attachment

This day came the Plaintiffs by his attorney Harry L. Douglass

(p 88)   Records & Judgements of June term 1815.
Pleas at the Court house in Lebanon &.

MATHEW FIGURES Plft.)
        VS   )   In Debt
WILLIAM C. TUCKER Deft.)

        Be it remembered that heretofore to wit at December term 1814 a
writ issued thus, State of Tennessee W̶i̶l̶s̶o̶n̶ ̶C̶o̶u̶n̶t̶y̶
        To the Sheriff of Wilson County Greetings:
        You are hereby commanded to take the body of William C. Tucker
if to be found in your county and him safely keep so that you have him
before the justice of our court of pleas and quarter sessions to be held
for the County of Wilson at the court house in the town of Lebanon on the
3rd Monday in March next then & there to answer Mathew Figures of a plea
that he render to him three hundred dollars, which to him he owes and from
him unjustly detains to his damage one hundred dollars. Herein fail not
and have you then there this writ, witness John Allcorn Clerk of our said
court at office this third Monday in December A.D. 1814 and in the 39th
year of American Independence.
                        John Alcorn Clerk.
        I acknowledge myself the above plaintiffs security in the sum of
two hundred dollars for prosecuting the above writ with effect or payment
of all costs and damages to the defendant on failure thereof witness my
hand and seal this 2nd day of Feby. 1815.
                        H.L. Douglass C.P.

        Issued the 2nd Feby. 1815
        Came to hand the same day issued 2nd Feby. 1815 not found.
                        Thomas Bradley S.W.C.

(p 89) at said March term 1815 the following rule of court is made to wit,
It is ordered by the court that a judicial attachment issue returnable
to next court which issued thus.

STATE OF TENNESSEE)
WILSON COUNTY COURT)
To the Sheriff of said County Greetings:
        Whereas MathewFigures of said county instituted his action of debt
against a certain William C. Tucker for the sum of three hundred dollars
and on the 2nd day of February 1815 the writ issued. Which writ you made
return thereof to March term 1815 of said court (thus
        Came to hand the same day issued 2nd Feby. 1815 not found.
                        T. Bradley S.W.L.
whereupon a rule of court was made for a judicial attested to issue.
        These are therefore to command you to attach the estate of the
said William C. Tucker if to be found in your county or so much thereof
repleviable on security as shall be of value sufficient to satisfy the
said the said debt and costs that may accrue thereon according to com-
plaint- and such estate so attached in your hands to secure or otherwise
to provide so that the same may be liable to further proceedings thereupon
to be had at the insuing court of pleas and quarter sessions to be held
for the county of Wilson at the court house in Lebanon on the third Monday
in June next so as to compel the said William C. Tucker to appear and
answer the above complaint and have you then and there this writ and make

known how you have executed this writ. Witness John Allcorn, clerk of said court at office this third Monday in March 1815 and in the 39th year of American Independence.

John Allcorn Clk.

Issued the 7th June 1815. Came to hand the same day issued and levied on one thin knife given as (p 90) given as the property of William C. Tucker.

T. Bradley S.W.C.

At June term 1815 came the plaintiff by H.L. Douglass Esquire his attorney & filed his declaration within the first three days of the term in the words & figures to wit.

STATE OF TENNESSEE) June term 1815
WILSON COUNTY COURT)

Mathew Figures by his attorney complains of William C. Tucker who is attached && of a plea that he render to him three hundred dollars which to him he owes and from him unjustly detains. For that the said William C. on the 16th day of March 1813 at the County aforesaid made his certain writing obligatory sealed with his seal and signed with his name & to the court now here sworn therein undertook & promised to pay the said plft. the said sum of three hundred dollars on or before the 25th day of December next the then next following, Yet the said William C. hath not paid said sum of money or any part thereof altho often requested but hath and still doth refuse to the Plaintiffs damage one hundred dollars & therefore he sues &&.

Douglass atto.

The defendant being solemnly called & failing to appear and plead within the limit allowed by law nor is any defence made whereupon it is considered by the court that the plaintiff aforesaid recover against the said Defendant three hundred dollars the debt in the decleration mentioned also the sum of twenty seven dollars damages by way of interest by the detention of said debt amounting also his cost $327 of suit in this behalf expended && - (p 91) & that the property attached be first sold for this judgement &&.

THOMAS WILLIAMSON PLFT.)
        VS   ) Debt
ADAM VINEYARD DEFT.   )

This day came the deft. by his attorney and the plaintiff failing to appear and file his decleration or otherwise claim his demant on motion of said defendants attorney, It is ordered by the court that the plaintiffs suit be dismissed and that the deft. recover against the plaintiff his costs of suit in this behalf expended &&.

JOHN ALLCORN Plft.)
        VS   ) In Debt
JOHN YOUNG Deft   )

This day came the plaintiff by his atto. and the said defendant in proper person comes into court and acknowledged the plaintiff action for one hundred and twenty nine dollars and thirty four cents. It is therefore considered by the court that the said plaintiff recover against the said deft. the said sum of one hundred and twenty nine dollars and thirty four cents the debt by the defendant confessed including interest

also his cost of in this be-half expended & the said defendant in mercy
&&. 27th April 1816.

      Recd. payment of J. Young in full Cr. by 85 Do. 2nd Febry. 1816
Cr. by $85 dollars in this Judt.

JOSEPH COTE Plft.)
      VS   )   Issue alias Issued
JOHN TRICE Deft.)

(p 92) Records of Judgement at June Term 1815

THOMAS BRADLEY Plft.)
      VS   )   Case Contd.
SAMUEL MEREDITH Deft.)

JANE CRAYTON Plft.   )
      VS   ) Tresspass - Decleration filed
EZEKIEL BASS & Wife Deft.)

      Deft by their attorney pleads not guilty justification statute of
limitation issue to the just plea replication & issue to the courts contd.

SAMUEL BOOKER Plft.)
      VS   ) Tresspass
WILLIAM CROSS Deft.)
      Plead and try at next term.

MICHAEL WILSON Plft.)
      VS   ) Appeal
ALLEN RACKLY Deft.)

      This day came the parties by their attornies also a jury of
good and lawful men to wit, Dennis Kelly, Yard Sellars, John Johnson,
Thomas Carver, Ryland Chandler, Mulberry Horn, Starling Tarpley, James
Welch, Charles Cox, Thomas Error

THOMAS WILSON   )
      VS   ) In Debt
TEPHIMAN NEIL Deft.)

      This day came the plaintiffs by his attorney and filed his declera
tion within the time prosecuted by law, and the defendant failing to appear
and plead or defend the plaintiffs (p 93) action, It is therefore considered by the court that the plaintiff recover against the deft. according
to specialty with interest amounting to one hundred and one dollars and
five cents the amount of debt and interest & and the deft. also his cost
of suit in this be-half expended &&. Third day of the term.

STATE   ) Seth P. Pool prosecuted
    VS   ) T.A. Battery plea not guilty
JOHN BONNER)

      This day came the State counsel also a jury of good and lawful
men to wit, William Draper, William Irwin, James Turner Solomon Williams
Samuel Motheral, John Ferrington, William Oakly, Coleman Stone, Jonathan
Ozement, Isham Jackson, Samuel Farmer, & Robert Irwin, who being elected

tried and sworn the truth to speak upon the issue of travers upon their oaths do say they find the defendant is guilty as charged in the bill of Indictment but leave it with the court to assess the fine whereupon it is considered by the court that the said defendant be fined the sum of one cent and that the state recover her cost in this prosecution &&.

Chantlocks, a witness 3 days
Jones Lock 2 days
William New 3 days
E. Mitchell 3 days
John M. Jackson 3 days
John C. Ligand, 1 day 36 miles 1 ferry

STATE)
HUMPHRY CHAPPLE) Indictment T.A.B.
        Deft. pleads not guilty

~~This day came the state by the solicitor and the defendant/also by his attorney/and~~

(p 94) Records of June Term 1815

STATE)
VS)
HUMPHREY CHAPPEL) Indict T. at B.
D. HANCOCK Prosecutor)

        This day came the state by the solicestors and the defendant by ~~his attorney and there upon came a jury of good and lawful men to wit~~ and being charged as in the bill of Indictment pleads guilty to the charge & puts himself upon the mercy of the court. The court after hearing the evidence in behalf of the state as well in behalf the defendant are of opinion the defendant be fined the sum of twenty dollars and imprisoned until the fine be paid also all cost in this behalf expended. The defendant came into court and paid the said fine of twenty dollars. It is therefore ordered that he be discharged. Henry Reed, a witness for the state proved 3 days.
Samuel Irwin, do proved 3 days &&.

STATE)
  VS) Indict. Jas Hill prosecutor.
SHADRACK GREGG)
        The Defendant pleads not guilty -

        This day came the state by the solicitor & the defendant by his attorney and thereupon came a jury of good and lawful men to wit, Joseph Cole, Lard Sellars, Samuel Stuart, Milbey Hern, Ryland Chandler, Dennis Kelly, Thomas Conn, Sterling Tarply, John Johnson, Nolly Madox, Samuel Sherrill, & William Hickman, who being elected tried & sworn to well & truly try the issue joined upon their oaths do say the find the defendant not guilty as charged in the bill of Indictment. It is therefore the opinion of the court the defendant be discharged and on motion of (p 95) the solicitor It is considered by the court that the County Treasurer pay the cost of this prosecution out of any monies in the treasury not otherwise appropriated.

Wm. Draper a witness for the state 3 days attendance
James Moore   "   "   "   "   3 days attendance
Alexander Patterson   "   "   "   3 days attendance
Anthony Seals a witness for deft.   3 days
John Cox   "   "   "   3 days
Patsy Grigg   "   "   "   1 day
John Grigg   "   "   "   1 day
Edward Moore   a witness for the state 3 days
Lewis Griffin   "   "   defendants 3 days
Tavernr Spradley   "   "   "   3 days

STATE   )
    VS   )   Recognizances- H. Chappel prosecutor
BATCHELOR GRAVES)

        This day the prosecutor and also the defendant who submits to the
mercy of the court. It is therefore considered by the court that the
defendant be discharged from his recognizance but that the state recover
his costs in this behalf expended &&.

STATE   )
    VS   )   Indictment T.A.B.
JAMES SHAW & WIFE)

        The defts. being charged pleads not guilty &&. Justices present
C. Cooper, I. Henderson, M. Davis, T.B. Rey.

        This day came the state by the county solicitor and also the
defendants by their counsel and thereupon came a jury of good and lawful
men to wit. Dennis Kelly, Joseph Cole, Samuel Stuart, Lard Sellars, John
Johnson, Thomas Carver, Ryland Chandler, Melbry Hern, (p 96) Sterling
Tarpley, Samuel Irwin, Will Parrish, James Eason, who being elected tried
& sworn the truth to speak upon the issue of Traverse wherein the state
is plaintiff & James Shaw & wife defendants upon their oaths do say they
defendants are guilty as charged in the bill of Indictment. It is therefore considered by the court that the defendant be fined the sum of fifty
dollars and be committed to close jail until the same is paid also the
state recover her cost of prosecution. The defts came into court & paid
the fine of fifty dollars, It is ordered that execution issue for the
costs.
Mrs. Turnham a witness for the state   3 days
Mrs. Hickman "   "   "   "   "   3 days
Lot Joiner   "   "   "   "   "   3 days
Anderson Trice   "   "   "   "   3 days
James Monet A   "   "   Defts   1 day

STATE   )
    VS   )   Recognizance
ALEXANDER CAPPS)
        The Defendant being called comes into court, pleads guilty and
submits to the mercy of the court, It is thereupon considered by the
court that the said defendant be fined the sum of five dollars and cost
of suit fine & costs said by the defendant &&.

STATE   )
    VS   )   Presentment - Caps to issue
JAMES D. WALKER)

(p 97) Quarter sessions began & held for the County of Wilson at the court house in the town of Lebanon on Monday the 18th day of Sept. 1815 & the 40th year of Am. Independence. Present, William Steele, Joseph T. Williams, James Henderson & Walter Carruth, justices who took their seats & proceeded to business.

The following persons were elected as a grand jury to wit, Moses Thompson, foreman, Beverly Williams, Isaac Hunter, Reuben Searcy, Jacob Ellis, Hugh Bradley, Jordan Ward, Lawrence Sypert, Giles Bowers, Allen Ross, Matheas Hauk, Mathew Horn & James Prim who being charged sworn and sent to inquire for the body of the county &&.

James Carruth a constatable sworn to attend the grand jury -

```
JAMES WINCHESTER & CO.    )
         VS               )
OBY SPRADLIN ADM. LARKIN  )    Case
ECHOLS DECEASED Deft.     )
```

Justices present Joseph J. Williams, Isham F. Davy, John Williams and Isaac Winston.

On the 19th day of September 1815 came the parties by their attornies and thereupon came a jury of good and lawful men, to wit, William Lawrence, Abraham Cooper, Abner Bone, Isaac Moore, James Scoby, Bradford Howard, Coleman Stone, Isham Palmer, John Alexander, John Harpole, Charles Lock & Henry Howel, who being elected tried and sworn the truth to speak upon the issue joined upon their oaths do say they find the pleas in favor of the plaintiff as set forth in this decleration and that the defendant hath not paid the said debt of one hundred dollars nor any part thereof as the said plaintiff in declaring hath alledged and assess the plaintiffs damages by the detention of said debt to forty dollars & forty cents. It is therefore considered by the court that the said plaintiff recover against the said deft. (p 98) one hundred dollars for his debt also forty cents for his damages as by the jury aforesaid assessed also his costs of suit in that behalf expended.

No. 1. Motion by defts counsel for a new trial an argument had thereon, It is considered by the court that a new trial be granted the defendant.

```
JOEL MANN Plft. )
        VS      )    Case
CLACK STONE Deft)
        Continued under former rule
```

```
CORNELIUS JOINER Plft.)
         VS           )    Case
RICHARD MARLOW Deft.  )
```

Justices present, Christopher Cooper, James Cross, & Hugh Raven Esqrs.

On this 21st day of September 1815 came the parties by their attornies also a jury of good and lawful men, to wit, William Laurence, Abraham Cooper, Abner Bone, Isaac Moore, James Scoby, Bradford Howard, Isaac Hunter, Hugh Bradley, Allen Ross, Reuben Searcy, Giles Bowers, and Moses Thompson who being elected tried and sworn the truth to speak upon the issue joined upon their oaths do say they find /p/ the defendant is not guilty in manner and form as the plaintiff against him hath complained. It is therefore considered by the court that the deft. go hence without day and that he recover against the said plaintiff his cost of suit in this behalf expended &.

Mathew Scoby proved 8 days 79 miles 6 ferriages.
Levi Howell proved 4 days
Beverly Williams 4 days
John Lenny proved 6 days
John Brown 4 days
Adam Myers 6 days
George Smith 4 days
Arch L. Wood 4 days
James Pickeral 3 days those proved as witnesses in the above cause.

(p 99)

BLOODWORTH Lessee Plft.)
          VS   ) Eject. Contd. by consent
JAMES CRAWFORD Deft.   )

Andrew Castleman a witness proved 1 days attendance & 60 miles traveling
Robert Thompson   do 2 days 72 miles
John Rice 2 days
David Rice 2 days

JACOB LASSETER Lessee Plft.)
          VS   ) Eject. Cond. by consent
THOMAS STUART Deft   )

       William Jones a witness proved three days.
Jesse Rhodes a witness proved 3 days.

WILLIE/BLOUNT/GOVENOR/PLFT   )
          VS   ) Covt.
PETER/TURNER/&/JACOB/THOMAS/WFT.)

       Justices present Christopher Cooper, Joseph T. Williams, Diveraux Wynne, & James Henderson Esquire &.

       This day came the parties by their attornies also a jury of good and lawful man to wit, Coleman Stone, Beverly Williams, Jacob Ellis, Jordan Ward, Lourence Sypert, Mathias Hauk, Matthew Horn, James Prim, Peter Rogers, William Hardin, Soloman Williams, & Jesse Donnell, who being elected tried and sworn the truth to speak upon the issue joined upon their oaths do say the find the defendants has not paid the debt of twelve hundred dollars in the plaintiffs decleration mentioned and assess the plaintiffs damages occasioned by the detention of his debt to one hundred and twenty eight dollars seventy one cents, It is therefore considered by the court that the said plaintiff recover against the said defendants the said sum of twelve hundred dollars for his debt also one hundred & twenty eight dollars seventy one cents his damage by the jury aforesaid assessed which may be discharged.

(p 100)   Records of Sept. Term 1815.

WILLIE BLOUNT Governor successor & Deft)
                    VS   )
BENJAMIN TARVER & JACOB THOMAS Deft.   )

Justices present Christopher Cooper, Joseph T. Williams, Deveraux Wynne,
& James Henderson, Esquire on the 21st day of September 1815 came the partys
by their attornies also a jury of good and lawful men to wit Coleman Stone,
Beverly Williams, Jacob Ellis, Jordan Ward, Laurence Sypert, Matheas Hauk,
Matthew Horn, James Prim, Peter Rogers, William Hardin, Solomon Williams,
and Jesse Donnell who being elected tried and sworn the truth to speak upon
the issue joined upon their oaths do say they find ~~for~~ they defendants
hath not kept their covenant with the Plaintiff but hath broken the same
as the Plaintiff in his declaration hath alledged & after his damages to
twelve hundred dollars &&.
~~the plaintiff in his declaration who hath alledged~~
            It is therefore considered by the court that the said plaintiff
recover against the Defendant the said sum of twelve hundred dollars by
the jury aforesaid assessed ~~also his~~ costs of suit in that behalf
expended and the plaintiff by his attorney remits one sixth part of the
damages amounting to two hundred dollars it being the widows distributive
share && and the defts in mercy &&

ISAAC HILLARD & WIFE Plft.)
              VS   ) Tresspass
WYATT BETTIS Deft.   )

            Edmund Crutcher and Joseph Johnson to whom this suit was refered
report as follows, They find in favour of the Plaintiff fifty cents besides
his costs. It is therefore considered by the court that the said Plaintiff
the said sum of fifty cents for his damages also his cost as by the arbitrators awarded Thomas Harrington Senr. Thomas Harrington Jr. and Charles
Harrington proved two days each.

(p 101)

JOHN B. GATHNEY Plft.)
              VS   ) Certiorari Contd.
ROSS WEBB Deft.   ) Issue alias writ of Certain

THOMAS BRADLEY Plft.)
              VS   ) Case Decleration
SAMUEL MEREDITH Deft.) Deft. Pleas.

Non assumpset set off & statute of limitations && Rep. & issue

JANE CRAYTON Plft.)
              VS   ) Tresspass
DRED BASS & WIFE Deft.)

            This day came the parties by their attornies who agree that the
award made by the arbitrators mutually chosen be exhibited in court and
stand as the judgement of this court which award is in the following words
and figures to wit,

STATE OF TENNESSEE)
WILSON COUNTY   )

We whose names are hereunto subscribed & seals affixed being indifferently chosen arbitrators to settle a matter of controversy & dispute between Richard Womack Sen. and Dreddin Bass, having carefully examined the witnesses and duly considered the testimony on both sides of the said parties for the settleing amity and friendship between them make and publish this our award by and between the said parties in the following manner to wit, whereas Nancy Bass has charged Jane Crayton a daughter of Richard Womack's with having a bastard child and not being able to support the said charge we do award and say that Driddon Bass shall pay all cost in any wise relating to or concerning the said premises and (p 102) and we do award and order that all actions, suits, quarrels, and controversies whatsoever arison depending between the said parties in law or equity as touching the said premises to the present date hereof shall cease and be no further prosecuted.

Given under our hands & seals this thirteenth day of Sept. 1815.

Thomas B. Beem
John W. Payton
Samuel Cannon arbitrators

It is therefore considered by the court that the said Plaintiff recover against the said defendant his cost of suit as the arbitrators hath awarded &&.

SAMUEL BOOKER Plft.)
        VS   ) Tresspass
WILLIAM CROSS Deft.)

Be it remembered that heretofore to wit, at June Term 1815 William Cross was attached to answer Samuel Booker of a plea of Tresspass in the case to his damage two hundred dollars at ssaid term a rule was made to plead & try at next term at September Term 1815 came the Plaintiff by his attorney Harry L. Douglass Esquire and filed his decleration in the following words and figures viz Wilson County State of Tennessee Leb. September term 1815. Samuel Booker by his attorney complains of William Cross in custody && in a plea of the case to his damage of two hundred dollars for that whereas the said deft. on ----- at Lebanon in Wilson aforesaid being possessed of a (p 103) certain brown mare which was unsound and infected with a bad and internal disorder or distemper to wit, the glanders which rendered the said brown mare good for nothing. And the Plaintiff being then and there possessed also of another sorrel mare of his own property of the value of two hundred dollars he the said defendant to induce the plaintiff to swap and exchange his sorrel mare did then & there faulsly & fradulently afirm to the plaintiff most positively that his the said defendants brown mare as far as he knew was then well, good sound healthy & clear of any disorder or distemper whatever - thereup the plaintiff giving full credit and belief to the said defts assertions and affirmation was instantly induced to and did then and there deliver his said sorrel mare to the said defendant in swap & exchange for the said defendants brown mare and the said defendant did them and there also deliver his said brown mare aforesaid and also then & there declare and affirm to the said plaintiff that the said brown mare was sound & Healthy as aforesaid now the plaintiff in fact says that the said defendants brown mare aforesaid was not at the time of the swap exchange delivery assertions affirmation & aforesaid were good sound healthy and clear of any disorder or distemper but that the said Brown mare was then (p 104) and there unsound infected & laboring under a bad & internal disorder or distemper to wit. The glanders of which he afterwards to wit at Lebanon aforesaid on then & there died without ever having rendered the plaintiff any services or benefit of all of which the said defendant was then and there knowing. And so the said Defendant by the means of his several faults & fradulent assertions & affirmation has greatly injured defrauded & indamaged the plaintiff to wit to the amount of two hundred dollars and he therefore brings his suit.

Douglass attorney for Plaintiff.

A second court for warrantee.

And the said defendant by his attorney comes and defends the wrong & injury then &&. and every thing else he ought to defend and for plea says said plaintiff his action aforesaid against him ought not to have & maintain because he says he is not guilty of the fraud and deceit as said plaintiff in declaring hath alledged against him and of this he puts himself on the county.

L. Anderson attorney

And the plaintiff doth the same.

At said September Term 1815, came the parties by their attornies also a jury of good and lawful men to wit, William Laurence, Abraham Cooper, Abner Bone, Isaac Moore, James Scoby, Bradford Howard, Isaac Hunter, Hugh Bradley, Alen Ross, Reuben Siroy, Giles Bowers, & Moses Thompson, who being elected tried and sworn the truth to speak upon the issue (p 105) joined upon their oaths do say they find for the defendant is not guilty of the fraud and deceit as charged in the plaintiffs declaration in manner and form as against the Plft. hath alledged &&. It is therefore considered by the court that the Plaintiff Defendant go hence without day and recover against the plaintiff his cost of suit in this behalf expended & motion by the plaintiffs attorney for a new trial which is granted by the court and given remit &&.

Uriah Cross a witness proved 4 days witness
James Cross a witness proved 4 days witness
Thomas Bone   "   "   4 days   "
Robert Alexander "   "   4 days   "
John Alexander   "   "   4 days
Thomas Henry   "   "   4 days   "

WILLIAM MOORE Plft.)
    VS   ) Covenant
WILLIAM WORD Deft.)

Justices present Joseph T. Williams, James Henderson, Hugh Roane & Deveraux Wynne, Esquires.

Be it remembered that heretofore towit at June Term 1815 William Word was attached to answer William Moore in a plea of covenant broken to his damage five hundred dollars. And at said June Term came the plaintiff by his attorney William Hadly esquire and filed his decleration in the following words & figures to wit.

STATE OF TENNESSEE)
WILSON COUNTY   ) June Term 1815

     William Moore, by his (p 106) his attorney complains of William
Werd in custody && of a plea of covenant on the eleventh day of March
1815 to wit in the county aforesaid made & executed to the said plaintiff
his own proper name & sealed with his seal and which is now here shown
to the court the date whereof is the same day and year aforesaid by which
said covenant said defendant amongst other things covenanted and agreed
with said Plaintiff that a certain negro slave named Rier about seventeen
years of age then & there granted sold and delivered to the said plaintiff
and warranted her the said Rier to be a healthy sound negro. Nevertheless
the said defendant hath not kep & performed his said covenant made as
aforesaid but hath broken the same in this to wit that the said negro
girl slave named Rier was not a healthy sound negro but said negro girl
slave was then & had been for some time before the date of said covenant
subject to fits and divers other diseases and still continues to labor
under fits & divers others diseases so that said negro girl slave is
rendered who by useless and unfit service by reason whereof said defendant
hath broken his covenant aforesaid to wit in the county aforesaid in the
day & year aforesaid to the damage of the plaintiffs five hundred dollars
& therefore he sues &&.
               Wm. Hadly atto.
               P. 2

     And at the term aforesaid and within the three days of the term
the defendant by his attorney Harry L. Douglass esquire enters the following
pleas on the docket to wit. Covenant performed non infregit with leave
to plead specialty Rep. & Issue.

(p 107) Records of September Term 1815.
     At September term 1815 came the parties by their attornies and
also a jury of good and lawful men to wit, Coleman Stone, Beverly Williams,
Jacob Ellis, Jordan Ward, Lawrence Sypert, Matheas Hauk, Mathew Horn,
James Prim, Soloman Williams, Jesse Donnell, James T. Wynne and John W.
Nichols, who upon their oaths do say the find the defendant hath not kept
and performed in covenant as the plaintiff in his declaration hath alledged
and assess the plaintiffs damages occasioned by the said bunch of covenant
to three hundred & forty five dollars sixty & two third cents. It is
therefore considered by the court that the said plaintiff recover against
the said defendant the sum of three hundred and forty five dollars seventy
& two third cents for his damages as by the jury aforesaid in form aforesaid assessed also his costs of suit in this behalf expended &&. From
which judgement the defendant prays an appeal to the next Circuit Court
to be held for the County of Wilson on the first Monday in March next
upon the said Defendants filing reasons entering into bond with Leonard
H. Sims & James Cross, securities an appeal is granted him &&.

(p 108) Records of Sept. Term 1815.

JOHN W. LUMPKIN Plft.)
       VS   ) Motion
JOSEPH CASTLEMAN Deft.)

     This day came the plaintiff by his attorney and also a jury of good and lawful men to wit Coleman Stone, Beverly Williams, Jacob Ellis, Jordan Word, Lawrence Sypert, Matheas Hauk, John Marshall, James Prim, Soloman Williams, Jesse Donnell, Jas T. Wynne, and John W. Nicholas, who being elected tried and sworn the truth to speak whether or not John W. Lumpkin was or was not the security of Joseph Castleman, in a note given to William Moore, upon which the said Moore recovered Judgement at June term 1815 who upon their oaths do say they find John W. Lumpkins to be the security of Joseph Castleman in a Note ~~given to William Moore upon which the said Moore received Judgement at June Term 1815 who upon their oaths do say they find John W. Lumpkin to be the security of Joseph Castleman, in a note upon~~ which Judgement was recovered by William Moore at June term 1815 and further found for the sum of one hundred and sixty Dollars and twenty five cents- and further say they find that eighty four dollars sixty two cents has been out of the said John W. Lumpkin, the balance of said debt & costs It is therefore considered by the court that the said John W. Lumpkin recover against the said Joseph Castleman, the said sum of eighty four dollars sixty two cents for his debt as by the Jury aforesaid assessed also his cost of this motion &c.

And that he have his execution as the Defts. property &c.

(P-109)

DAWSON HANCOCK PLFT.	) T.&A.
VS	) Battery
HUMPHY CHAPPEL DEFT.	)

Dismissed by Plft.

WILLIAM HALLEMAN &	)
Wife PLFT.	) T.
VS	) A. B.
JAMES SHAW &	)
Wife DEFT.	)

This day came the parties into court and agree that this has been left to reference and that the well abide by the award which should be the Judgement of the Court.

And the award being exhibited in Court in the following words and figures To wit September the 7th 1815 we John W. Lumpkin, Jehu Ferrington, Richard Robertson, has agreed that the Defendant Shaw shall pay all the cost and five dollars Damages, to the said Halluman Given under our hands & seals the 7th of Sept. 1815 John W. Lumpkin, Jehu Ferrington, Jonathan Ozment, Robt. Robertson, (Seals),   It is therefore considered by the Court that the Plaintiff recover against the said Defendant the sum of five dollars as by the arbitrators awarded also his cost in that behalf expended &.

JOHN HARPOLE PLFT.	)
VS	) Debt Declaration
Wm. ALLIN &	) filed 2nd day
JNO. GOLDSTON, DEFT.	) pleas payment & set off Repl. & issue.

JAMES McDANIEL PLFT GUARDIAN	)
VS.	) Trespass
ABRAHAM PRIM DEFT.	) Issue Alias writ.

JAMES McFARLEN PLFT.)
       VS   ) DEBT
WILLIAM MORTON DEFT.) ISSUE ALIAS WRIT

(P-110)

BENJAMIN MOTLEY PLFT.)
       VS   ) Debt
JOHN W. NICHOLS DEFT.) Dect. filed

       Pleas payment set off and no assignments to the plaintiff
                 Rept. & Issue

BURWELL MOSLEY PLFT.)
       VS   ) Debt plead & try at Next term so as not
J. KELLY &   ) to Delay trial.
H. DONELSON   DEFT.)

THOMAS WILSON, PLFT.)
       VS   ) Debt Du.
JOSE ECHOLS &   )   filed
R. ANDERSON   DEFT.)

2nd day pleas payment set off Rept & issue

JOSEPH COLE PLFT.)
       VS.   ) Sciri facias
JOHN TRICE JUNIOR DEFT)

(P-111)

LEMUEL WRIGHT PLFT.)
       VS   ) Debt
BLAKE RUTLAND DEFT.) Plead & try at next term so as not to

Delay the trial &c.

WILLIAM EDWARDS PLFT.)
       VS   ) Trespass F.
SAMUEL ALSUP   DEFT.) important
                 Declaration filed

       The Defendant to plead and try next court so as not to delay the
trial.

JOHN DEN LESSEE   )
WILLIAM CROSS, PLFT.)
       VS.   ) In Eject
JONATHAN PHILLIPS DEFT.) Decl. filed 2nd day

Defendant enters into the common rule & Plead not guilty-
& Issue

THOMAS RICHMOND PLFT.   )
      VS.   ) Debt
JOHN W. NICHOLAS DEFT.   ) Decl. filed 2nd day &c.

Pleas payment set off no assignment from Robert Bumpass, to John W.
Lumpkins Reps. & issue.

ROBERT DONELSON PLFT.)
     VS   ) Case
EDMUND GREENAGE DEFT   ) Issue Alias

SAMUEL ELLIOTT PLFT.)
     VS   ) In Debt
JOHN W. LUMPKIN DEFT.)

The Defendant in proper person comes into Court and confesses the
plaintiffs action of Debt against him for three hundred and sixty six
dollars with interest from the 5th day of Sept. 1815 Amounting one dollar
20 cents It is there fore considered by the Court that the plaintiff
recover against the defendant the Debt and Interest as by the the Defendant Confessed amounting to three hundred & sixty seven dollars &
twenty cents also his costs of suit &

(P-112)

STATE   PLFT   )
   VS   ) Indictment
JAMES D. WALKER DEFT.)

This day came as well William Williams, Esq. the County solicitor as
the Defendant James D. Watkins, by his attorney And thereupon came a
jury of good and lawful men to wit William Lawrence, Abraham Cooper,
Abner Bone, Isaac Moore, James Scoby, Bradford Howard, Coleman Stone,
Isham Wynne, William Bass, Uriah Cross, William Melone, & Henry Howel,
who being elected tried and sworn the truth to speak upon the issue
Joined upon their oaths do say that the said James is not guilty as in
pleading he hath alledged- Therefore it is considered by the Court that
the said Defendant be discharged and that he go hence & on Motion It
is considered by the Court that the prosecution was Matusions & that the
prosecutor William Stuart be taxed with all costs Accd that have or
may accrue in said prosecution

    Charles Blaylock a witness proved 1 day
    James Lisseem a witness for Deft. 1 day
    Noah Walker   "   "   " 1 day
    Sally Crossland "   "   " 1 day
    Beverly Williams "   "   " 1 day

Ordered that Court adjourn until Court in course as Edmond Crutcher, Jas. T. Williams, Joseph Johnson, & James Davidson Esquires.

(P-113)   Blank

(P-114)   Please before the Court of pleas & quarter sessions held for the County of Wilson at the Court house in Lebanon on the 3rd Monday in December 1815 being the 18th day of month.

```
JAMES WINCHESTER & CO  PLTF. ) )
            VS                )   Tresspass
OBEDIAH SPRADLIN Administrator )   on the
of LACKEW ECHOLS Decd. DEFT.  )   Case
```

Be it remembered that here to fore to wit at June term 1814 Obediah Spradlin, Administrator of Lacken Echols decd. was attached to answer James Winchester & Company in a plea of tresspass on the case to these damages one hundred and fifty dollars &c
    At said June term a rule of Court thus
    Plead and try at next term

At September term 1814 came the Plaintiffs by their Attorney Joseph W. Armstrong, Esquire and filed their decleration in the following words & figures to wit.

```
STATE OF TENNESSEE    )
WILSON COUNTY         ) September Term 1814
```

James Winchester, William Cage and Thomas Wilson trading under the firm of James Winchester, & Company by their attorney complains of Obediah Spradlin, Administrator of the goods & chattels rights and credits of Lacken Echols deceased in Custody &C. in a plea of tresspass on the case, For that whereas the said Lacken Echols, in his life time on the 17th day of May 1808 towit in the County aforesd. (P-115) Aforesaid by his certain endorsment in writing on the back of a certain writing obligatory/^{or} bill single signed with the proper name and sealed with the seal of a certain Elisha Brown, by which the said Elisha Brown promised and bound himself to pay to said Larkin Echols on or before the 25th day of December 1808 the sum of one hundred dollars for value received, and dated the 29th day of December 1806 assigned the said Bill Single to Benjamin Tarver for value recd. and signed with the proper names and sealed with seal of the said Lacken and afterwards to wit on the 18th day of May 1808 in the County aforesaid the said Benjamin Tarver by his certain endorsement in writing on the back of the said Bill Single signed with his own proper name and sealed with his seal assigned the said note to the plaintiff - and the said plaintiff avers that afterwards to wit on the day of to wit in the County aforesaid the time for payment of said Bill Single being elapsed they presented said Bill Single in writing obligatory to the said Elisha Brown, and then and there requested the said Brown to pay them the amount thereof nevertheless the said Brown refused to pay said $100 or any part thereof to said plaintiff of which said Plaintiff afterwards to wit on the day of aforesaid to wit in the County aforesaid gave said Defendent notice, by reason whereof

and by virtue of the act of assembly in such case made & proveded said
Lacken in his life time and said defendant and as his administrator
since his death became bound   (P-116) and liable to pay said Plaintiff
said hundred dollars and so being bound and liable as aforesaid said
Defendant afterwards to wit on the last day and year aforesaid to wit in
the County aforesaid undertook & faithfully promised to pay said hundred
dollars when he should be thereto afterwards requested never theless
said Lacken in his life time nor said defendant since their decease of
the said Lacken hath not paid said one hundred dollars nor any part there
of the often requested to wit in the County aforesaid on the same last
days and year aforesaid, But to pay the same hither to hath wholly failed
and refused and still doth refuse the same to pay or any part there of to
the damage of the Plaintiffs one hundred & fifty dollars and therefore
they sue & .

Armstrong Atto. P 2.

And at said September Term aforesaid came the said Obediah Adminis-
tratory as aforesaid and defend the wrong & injury when &c and saith
that the said decleration and the matter there in contained are not
sufficient in law for plaintiff to have and maintain their said action
against him, to which decleration the said defendant hath no need nor is
he obliged by the law of the land to answer wherefore for want of a
sufficient decleration in this be-half the said defendant prays, Judgement, and that said Plaintiff may be barred from having & maintaining
their action there of against him Joined and demurred.

Douglass for Deft.

Armstrong & Anderson,
(P-117)   At December Term 1814
      Cont^d by consent
            At March Term 1815 came the said parties by their
Attornies and upon solemn argument had there on the demurrer of the
Defendant by the Court is overruled and a respondeas auster awarded
at June term 1815 the Defendant prays non assumpset to which plea the
plaintiffs joined issue &c at September term 1815 on the 19th day of
September 1815 Came the parties by their attornies and thereupon Came
a jury of good and lawful men to wit William Lawrence, Abraham Cooper,
Abner Bone, Isaac Moore, James Scoby, Bradford Howard, Coleman Stone,
Isham Palmer, John Alexander John Harpole, Charles Lock, and Henry
Howard, who being elected tried and sworn the truth to speak upon the
issue joined upon their oaths do say the find the pleas in favour of
the Plft. as set forth in their decleration, and that the defendant
hath not paid the said debt of one hundred dollars nor any part there of
as the Plaintiff in declaring hath alledged and assess the Plaintiffs
damages occasioned by the detention of said debt to forty dollars and
forty cents.
      It is there fore considered by the Court that they Plaintiff re-
cover against said Defendant one hundred dollars for his debt also forty
dollars & forty cents for his damages as by the Jury aforesaid assessed
also his costs of suit in this (P-118) this behalf expended.
      Motion by defendants Counsil for a new trial on argument had there-

on, It is considered by the court that a new trial be granted the Defendant &c.

At December term 1815 .

21st Dec. 1815 on this day came the parties by their attornies aforesaid also a jury of good and lawful men to wit Peter Leeth, Benjamin Spring, Josiah Smith, Robert Donelson, Thomas Dell, John Calhoon, William White, James Weir Sen. Samuel Henderson, George Alexander, John Dillon & Henry Shannon, who being elected tried and sworn the truth to speak upon the issue joined upon their oaths do say they find the Defendants intestate did not assume upon himself in manner and form as the Plaintiffs against him hath alledged It is therefore considered by the Court that the defendant go hence without day and recover against said Plaintiff their cost of suit in this behalf expended.

From which Judgement the Plfts. pray an appeal to the next Circuit Court to be holden for the County of Wilson at the Court house in Lebanon on the 1st Monday in March next. And upon entering into bond as the law directs & filing reasons It is ordered that an appeal be granted & .

    Costs $15.14

(P-119)

CLACK STONE Plf+ Deft.) VS) JOEL MANN PLFF)	Cont'd under former rule.

BLOODWORTH Lessee Plft) VS) JAMES CRAWFORD DEFT)	Eject Cont'd.

Andrew Castleman witness for the Plft. proved one days attendance & 60 miles traveling.

JACOB LASITER PLFT.) VS) THOS STUART DEFT.)	Eject.

on the 20th day of December 1815 Came the parties by their attornies also a jury of good and lawful men to wit John W. Nichols, Franklin Foster, Jesse C. Williams, Allen Backly, William Cross, John Adams, Thomas S. Green, John K. Wynne Brittian Drake, Jordan Reeves, Samuel Motheral, and Samuel R. Anderson, who being elected tried and sworn the truth to speak upon the issue joined upon their oaths do say they find the dependant is guilty of the tresspass and ejectment in manner and form as the Plaintiff in his decleration hath alledged and assess his damages to six and a fourth cents. It is there fore considered by the Court that the Plaintiff recover his term yet to come of and to the premises in his decleration mentioned, also 6¼ cents his damages by the jury aforesaid assessed and his cost of suit in this behalf expended & the plaintiff have his writ of posession & .

(P-120)	JOHN B. GOTHNEY) VS) ROSS WEBB)	Certiorari

On motion It is ordered by the Court that this cause to revived in the name of Elizabeth Webb, the administratrix of Ross Webb, dec^d. & cont^d. until next court.

THOMAS BRADLY PLFT.   )
        VS   ) Case
SAMUEL MEREDITH DEFT   )

Be it remembered that hereto-fore to wit at June Term 1815 Samuel Meredith one of the firm of Winchester,Cage and Meredith was attached to answer Thomas Bradley in a plea of tresspass on the case to his damage six hundred dollars.

At the term last aforesaid the rule of Court was this Plead and try next term or plead in abolement or demurer & try &c Contd.

At September Term 1815 Came the plaintiff by his attorney and filed his decleration in the words and figures to wit

STATE OF TENNESSEE   )
WILSON COUNTY LEB.   ) Sept. Term 1815

Thomas Bradley complains of Samuel Meredith, one of the firm of Winchester, Gage & Meredith in custody &c in a plea of trespass on the Case to his damage six hundred dollars For that whereas the said Samuel at Lebanon in Wilson aforesaid being indebted to the said Thomas in (P-121) in the aforesaid sum of six hundred dollars for so much money before that time had and received by the said Samuel to the use of the said Thomas inconsideration thereof then & there promised the Plaintiff to pay him the same on demand.

And for that whereas at Lebanon in Wilson aforesaid on the said Defendant was also indebted to the said Plaintiff in one other sum of six hundred dollars for so much money before that time lent loaned & accommodated by the said Plaintiff to the said Deft at his request and being so indebted in consideration there of afterwards, to wit on at undertook & faithfully promised to pay the same on demand to the said Plaintiff.

And for that whereas at Lebanon in Wilson aforesaid the said Defendant was indebted to the said plaintiff in one other sum of six hundred dollars for so much money before that time paid laid out and expended by the plaintiff for the use benefit & behalf of the said Defendant at his request and being so indebted in consideration there of afterwards to wit on at under-took and faithfully promised to pay the same on demand to the said Pft.

And that whereas at Lebanon in Wilson aforesaid the said Deft. and the said Plft. accounted together of and concerning their mutual dealings & of & concerning diverse sum of money before that time due from the Deft. to the plaintiff and there fore the said Defendant was found indebted to the said Plft. and in arrears in one other sum of six (P-122) six hundred dollars and being so indebted in consideration thereof afterwards to wit on at undertook and faithfully promised to pay the same on demand, yet the said Deft. though often requested has not paid the aforesaid sum of money or any part thereof but entending to deceive and defraud the said Plft. in this particular has hitherto wholly & still does refuse to pay the same or any part there of to his damage six hundred dollars and therefore he brings his suit.

Foster & Douglass Atto. for Plft.

Decleration filed the first day of said Term last aforesaid.
Deft. Pleads non assumpset set off & statute of limitations rep. & issue to the/two first pleas & specially to the last.

    Cont^d by consent.

    At December Term 1815
Came the parties aforesaid by their attornies also a jury of good & lawful men to wit. Samuel Elliott, Jordan Reeves, Brittain Drake, George Tucker, Richard Phelps, William Sypert, Charles Blaylock, Hezekiah Cartwright, William Word, Thomas Rhodes, William Adams, and Phillip Johnson, who being elected tried and sworn the truth to speak upon the issue joined upon their oaths do say they find the deft. did assume upon himself in manner and form as the Plaintiff in declaring hath alledged and assess the Plaintiffs damages by reason there of to twelve dollars and fifty cents &

    It is therefore considered (P-123) by the Court that the said Plft. recover against the said Defendant the sum of twelve dollars & fifty cents the damages aforesaid by the Jury aforesaid*also his cost of suit in this behalf expended & the Deft. in Mercy &c.

    From which Judgement the Plaintiff prays an Appeal to the next Circuit Court to be holden for the County aforesaid at Lebanon on the first Monday in March next. The said Plft. intered into bond as the law directs. Harry L. Douglass, his security upon reasons being filed &c. It is considered by the Court that an appeal be granted the Plaintiff & .

SAMUEL BOOKER	PLFT	)	
VS		)	Case
WILLIAM CROSS	DEFT.	)	Dismissed

each party paying one half the court costs — tax fee.
 to Plaintiff's attorney one half paid by each —

Each party to pay his own witness &c $3.41 cts. paid Plft. Booker $1.25 yet due it being one half the Plfts. lawyers tax fee &c 2nd January 1816.

* assessed

(P-124)	JOHN HARPOLE	PLFT	)	
	VS		)	In
	WILL ALLEN & JNO GOLDSTON	DEFT	))	Debt.

On this 21st day of December 1815 came the parties aforesaid by their attornies, also a jury of good and lawful men to wit Humphoys Donelson, David Garrett, John W. Nichols, Thos. C. Williams, Jordan Reves, Brittain Drake, Saml. Elliott, John K. Wynne, William Babb, Truman Modglin, Rowland Sutton, & Thomas Conyers who being elected tried and sworn the truth to speak upon the issue joined upon their oaths do say they find the said Defts. hath not paid the debt as the plaintiff in his declaration hath alladged and assess his damages occasioned by the detention of said debt to twenty five dollars and sixty ¢¢¢¢¢ four cents.

It is there fore considered by the Court that the plaintiff recover against the said defendants the sum of eighty five dollars seventy one and a half cents for his debt also twenty five dollars sixty four cents for his damages as by the Jury aforesaid assessed amounting in the whole to one hundred and twelve dollars twenty five and a half cents, also his costs of suit in that be half expended & the Defts in mercy &c. $112.35½ cts.

(P-125)

Benjamin Motley   Plft.)
VS   )   In
John W. Nichols   Deft.)   Debt

Pleas &c   Be it remembered   that here to fore to wit at September Term 1815 John W. Nichols, was attached to answer Benjamin Motley assignee of Joseph Castleman, of a plea that he render to him two hundred and fifty Dollars which to him he owes & from him unjustly detains to his damage one hundred dollars.

At said September term 1815 came the plaintiff by his attorney and filed his decleration in the following words and figures to wit.

STATE OF TENNESSEE   )
WILSON COUNTY   LEB.   )   September
term 1815   )

Benjamin Motly by his attorney complain of John W. Nichols, in custody & in a plea of that he render unto him two hundred & fifty dollars which to him he owes & from him unjustly detains For that whereas the said John W. Nichols, on the fourteenth day of November in the year 1814 at Lebanon in Wilson aforesaid by his Certain writing obligatory of that date sealed with his seal and here how in Court to be produced bound & acknowledged himself to be indebted to a certain Joseph Castleman in the aforesaid sum of money to be paid nine months after the date of said writing obligatory and the said Joseph afterwards and before the same was paid to wit in at Lebanon afoursaid by his endorsement on the back ofsaid writing obligatory his own proper hand thereto subscribed assigned the same to the said Plaintiff for value recd. of all of which the said Defendant then and there had notice and by force of the statute in such case (P-126) case made & provided became thereby liable to pay the same and an action has accured to the Plaintiff to sue for the same.

Yet the said Deft. tho. often requested has never yet paid the said sum of money or any part there of the time of payment being long since elapsed but wholly refuses so to do so his damage of one hundred dollars and there-fore he sues.

Douglass atto for the Plft.

And at the same term the defendant by his attorney plead payment and no
assignment to which there was replication & issue.

And now at this term to wit the term first above mentioned came
the parties by their attornies and also a jury of good and lawful men
to wit Jordan Reeves, Britton Drake, Samuel Elliott, Geo. Tucker, Jesse
C.,Williams, Jeremiah Tucker, Isaac Hunter, Henry Howell, William Babb,
Elias Cranford, John Marshall, Lewis Shepherd who being elected tried
and sworn the truth to speak upon the issue joined upon their oaths do
say they find the issue for the plaintiff and assess his damages to sixty
dollars & forty five cents it is there fore considered by the Court
that said plaintiff recover of the defendant his debt of one hundred and
fifty dollars with the damages aforesaid by the Jury aforesaid assessed
& also his cost by him about his suit expended.

(P-127)

BURWELL MOSLEY PLFT. VS.	) Debt	
KOLLY & DONNELSON, DEFT.	) Contd	
		) In
THOMAS WILSON PLFT. VS ECHOLS & ANDERSON DEFT.	) Debt.	

This day came the parties by their attornies also a jury of good
and lawful men to wit Humphy Donelson, Deverux Jarratt, John W. Nichols,
Thomas C. Williams, Jordan Reeves, Brittain Drake, Samuel Elliott, John
K. Wynne, William Babb, Truman Modglin, Rowland Sutton, and Thomas
Conyers, who being elected tried and sworn the truth to speak upon the
issue joined upon their oaths do say they find the Defendant hath not
paid the debt in the Plaintiffs declecation mentioned amounting to three
hundred sixty eight dollars forty cents a balance of his debt also twenty
dollars for his damages by way of interest. It is therefore considered
by the Court that the said plaintiff recover against the said Defendants
the sum of three hundred sixty eight Dollars and forty cents balance of
his debt also twenty dollars his interest by way of damages as by the
jury aforesaid assessed amounting in the whole to three hundred sixty
eight dollars and forty cents, also his costs of suit in this behalf expended & the defendants in mercy & .

WILLIAM EDWARDS PLFT	)
VS	) Tresspass
SAMUEL ALSUP, DEFT.	) & False mi
	Pressment

The Plaintiff comes into Court & prays his said suit Dismissed. and
the Defendant also comes into Court and assumes the costs It is therefore ordered by the Court the same be dismissed and that the Deft. pay

cost.

(P-128)

WILLIAM CROSS PLFT.   )   In
       VS   )   Ejectment
JONATHAN PHILLIPS DEFT.)

Cont'd Will Adams a witness proved 3 days

THOMAS RICHMOND   PLFT.)
      VS   ) In Debt.
JNO W. NICHOLS   DEFT)

This day came the parties by their attorneys also a jury of good and lawful men to wit, Jordan Reevis, Brittain Drake, Samuel Elliott, George Tucker, Isaac Hunter, Henry Howel, William Babb, Elias Crawford, John Marshall, & Lewis Sheppard, who being elected tried and sworn the truth to speak upon the issue joined who upon their oaths do say the find for the Defendant the plea of no assignment from Robert Bumpass to John W. Nichols as the Defendant in pleading hath alledged It is therefore Considered by the Court that the said defendant go hence with-out day and recover against the said plaintiff his costs of suit in this behalf expended &

Motion of the Plaintiff for a new trial It is the opinion of the Court that a new trial be granted the plaintiff at the next court on the third Monday in March in March next & .

(P-129)

CORNELIUS JOINER   PLFT.   )
      VS   )
DANIEL THYLMAN   )
MICAH VIVRETT & SION BASS   ) Motion
            DEFT.   )

This day came the said Cornelius by Ephriam H. Foster, his attorney and it appearing to the satisfaction of the court here that the said Cornelius has here to fore (to wit)   on the   day of   in the year   paid for the said Defts the sum of _____

Which said sum of money was received from and paid by the said Plaintf as appearance bail for the said Defts in a suit instuted in the Wilson County Court by Joseph M. Reynolds, against the said Defts - Therefore on motion consideration it is adjudged by the Court here that the said Cornelius do recover the aforesaid sum of money, paid as aforesaid for the use and benefit of said Defts according to the act of Assembly in suit case made & provided, to wit act entitled.

An Set to empower securities to recover damages in a summary way passed at the first session of the fourth general assembly of the State of Tennessee began and held at Knoxville on Monday the 21st of September in the year 1801.

And the Court here now give judgement for the said Plain # against the said Defts for the aforesaid sum of money and his costs of suit in this behalf expended and the Defts in mercy &

(P-130)

```
WILLIAM DONNEL    PLFT.  )
        VS               )
EMANUEL SEAT      DEFT.   )   Motion to Condemn
```

thirty one acres of land the property of Defendant levied on by virtue of an execution in favor of the Plaintiff It appearing to the Court that James Carruth a constable has levied an execution in favor of the plaintiff on 31 acres of land the property of said Deft. on the 2nd day of December 1815 lying in Jennings fork of Round Lick Creek near Carlings Springs adjoining to John Hales and Wm Perry's land therefore on motion of the plaintiff is considered by the Court that the said thirty one acres of land as above described be condemned and sold for the satisfaction of the plaintiffs balance of debt amounting to thirty four dollars & fifty cents, also cost of this motion & .

~~EMANUEL SEAT PLFT.~~
~~VS~~
~~MARTIN TALLY P~~

```
MARTIN TALLY     PLFTS. )   Motion to condemn
     VS                 )   50 acres of land
EMANUEL SEAT     DEFTS.     levied on by virtue of an execution.
```

It appearing to the court that an execution in favour of the Plaintiff for the sum of thirty two dollars and fifty cents for his debt also all lawful cost issued the 6th day of Dec. 1815. and that James Turner a constable has levied the same on fifty acres of land, the place whereon the said Emanuel Seat now lives thereupon the motion of the Plaintiff It is considered by the Court that the said fifty acres of land be condemned & sold for the satisfaction of the Plaintiffs debt also the cost of this motion &c.

(P-131)

```
MARTIN TALLEY PLFT.)
     VS           )   Motion
EMANUEL SEAT  DEFT.)
```

It appearing to the Court that on the 6th day of December 1815 an execution by Thos B. Reese Esquire in favour of the Plaintiff against the Defendant for the sum of eighty one dollars and fifty cents and it

further appearing to the Court that said execution is levied on fifty
acres of the officer returning no personal property found. It is therefore considered by the Court that the said fifty acres so levied on be
condemned and sold for the satisfaction of the said Debt, also the cost
of this motion &c.

Ordered that Court adjourn untill court in course

Edmund Crutcher J.P.
H. Shelby J.P.
O. G. Finley J.P.

(P-132-133 LEFT BLANK)

(P-134)

Pleas before the Court of Pleas & quarter sessions began and hold
for the County of Wilson at the Court house in Lebanon on the 18th Day
of March 1816 and 40th year of American Independence. Justices present
Christopher Cooper, Walter Carruth, & James Henderson, Esquirs who seated
themselves &proceeded to business.

No.1

JOEL MANN   PLFT.) Case
   VS   ) Contd. in
CLACK STONE   DEFT.) disform rule

BLOODWORTH   Lessee Plaintiff)
   VS   ) In
James Crauford   Deft.   ) Eject

The plaintiff comes into Court & says he intends no further to prosecute his said action of Ejectment against the Deft.

No.2

It is the ordered by the Court that his suit be dismissed and that
the Defen't go hence without day and recover his Costs in this behalf expended.

Robert Thompson a witness for the Plft. proved 1 days attendance &
72 miles travelling.
Andrew Castleman a witness for Plft proved 1 day 60 miles traveling
and 2 ferriges, Rend Clerks and Sheriffs fees $78.75

ROSS WEBB   PLFT   ) Certiorari
   VS   ) Continued.
JOHN B. GOTHNEY   DEFT.)

(P-135)

```
BURWELL MOSELY      PLFT.)
     VS                  ) Debt
KELLY & DONELSON    DEFT.)
```

This day came the parties by their attorneys also a jury of good and lawful men to wit John R. Wynne, James Mays, Isaac Williams, Reddick Eason, Baker Rather Robert Alexander, Henry Moser, William Word, James Leech, William A. Melone, John Gleeves, Melberry Hern, who being elected tried & sworn the truth to speak upon the issue joined upon their oaths do say the find the Defendants has not paid the debt in the plaintiffs decleration mentioned of two hundred and sixty four dollars and assess the the damages occasioned by the detention of said to twenty four dollars and forty one cents. It is therefore considered by the Court that the said plaintiff recover against the said Defendant the debt in in the Plaintiffs decleration mentioned also the damages aforesaid by the jury aforesaid assessed amounting in the whole to two hundred and eighty eight dollars & forty one cents. and that the Plfts have his execution &c.

```
5    WILLIAM CROSS   PLFT. ) Ejectment
          VS               ) stayed by
     JONATHAN PHILLIPS  DEFT) bill of
                            Injunction


     THOMAS RICHMOND PLFT )
          VS               ) In Debt.
6    JOHN W. NICHOLS  DEFT. )
```

This day came the parties by their attornies also a jury of good and lawful men to wit John K. Wynne, James Mays, Isaac William, Reddick Eason, Baker Rather, Robert Alexander, Henry Moser, William Word, James Leech, William A. Melone, John Gleves, & Milberry Hern, who being elected tried and sworn the truth to speak upon (P-136) the issued joined upon their oath do say the defendant has not paid the debt in the declaration mentioned of two hundred & twenty one dollars and assess his damages by reason thereof to ten dollars & nine cents It is therefore considered by the Court that the Plaintiff recover of said defendant the debt in the declaration mentioned together with the damages by the jury in form aforesaid assessed amounting to two hundred & thirty one dollars & nine cents and also his costs by him about his suit in this behalf expended.

```
ARON SOMERS      PLFT.      )
     VS                     )Appeal
BENTON MODGLIN   DEFT.      )
```

This day came the parties by their attornies and thereupon a jury of good & lawful men to wit Hezekiah Cartwright, John Gleeves, Joseph Cole, John Prestly, John N. Walker, Thomas Turnham, William Thomas, Jehu Ferrington, John Robb, James Parks, William Walker, Beverly Williams, who being elected tried and sworn well and truly to try the appeal between the parties aforesaid upon their oath do say they find for the defendant upon his plea of the statue against gaming, It is therefore considered by the Court that said defendant go hence & recover against said Plaintiff his costs by him about his defence in this behalf expended & that said Plft. &c.

(P-137)

```
        JOHN K. WYNNE & Other        )      )
Commissioners &c to sell the         )      )
negroes of PLEASANT HAILEY Decd. Plft.)     )
            VS                       )      )    Debt.
LEONARD H. SIMS, & THOS BRADLEY,     )      )
                        DEFT         )      )
```

The Defendants came into Court waves all errors and acknowledges themselves indebted to the Plaintiff John K. Wynne, & others in the sum of three hundred & forty five dollars the debt in the note of hand mentioned also three dollars forty five cents damages by way of interest amounting in the whole to three hundred & forty eight Dollars forty five cents It is there fore considered by the Court that the said Commissioners recover against the said Leonard H. Sims, & Thomas Bradley, the said sum of three hundred & forty eight dollars the debt and damages as by the said Defendant confessed also the cost of this Judgement.

```
7       ADAMS   Lessee  Plft.  )
            VS                 ) Ejectment
        ALLEN RACKLEY  Deft.   ) Stayed by
                    bill of Injunction


        BARKSDALE MARLOW   PLFT.  )
                VS                ) Case
        JAMES MARLOW       DEFT.  ) Contd


        WILLIAM GREEN      PLFT.  )
                VS                ) Certiorari
        JOHN JINKINGS      DEFT.  ) ++++++++++
```

This day came the parties by their attornies and thereupon on motion of the defendant by his attorney It is ordered by the court that the Plaintiffs Certiorari be dismissed and that said defendant recover against the plaintiff the sum of forty nine dollars and ninety nine cents the amount of Judgement rendered by the single justice with interest from the 16th of September 1815. Also his costs of suit in this behalf expended &c. from which Judgement the plaintiff in Certiorari prays an appeal to the next circuit Court to be held at the Court house in Lebanon on the first Monday in Sept. next which granted by the Court upon his intering to bond with security &c Josep Hamilton.

(P-138)   Records of March
        Term 1816

No
11

No SAMUEL CLEMNY PLFT.)
11   VS   ) Appeal
   JOHN McCAFFEE DEFT.) Continued

    DENNIS KELLY Plaintiff)
      VS   ) Motion
    JONATHAN PHILLIPS DEFT.)

(P-139)   Pleas before the Court of pleas & Quarter sessions began
& held for the County of Wilson at the Court house in the town of Lebanon
on this day the 17th day of June 1816 & 40th year of Am. Independence
Present the worshipful James Cross, Hugh Roam, & Edward Harris, Esquirs &
proceeded to business.

    JOEL MANN, PLFT) Case continued
     VS   )
    CLACK STONE DEFT) under firmer rule

   ROSS WEBB   Plaintiff)
No   VS   ) Certiorari
2 JOHN B. GOTHNEY Defendant)

   This day came the parties by their attornies and by mistrial consent
agrees this cause be continued, and if not arranged before next Court
that Judgement then be entered against the said John B. Gothney for costs
& It is therefore considered by the Court that this cause be continued.

No BARKSDALE MARLOW PLFT)
3   VS   ) Case
   JAMES MARLOW DEFT.)

   This day came the parties by their attornies and the plaintiff by
his attorney agrees to Dismiss his said action upon the Defendants agree-
ing to pay one half the cost, which is agreed to by the Defendant.

   It is there fore considered by the Court that this suit be dismissed and that each party pay half the cost and that execution issue for the
same &c.

   William Gleaves a witness proved 4 days attendance

   JOSIAH JONES PLFT)
4   VS   ) Covenant Contd. by Consent
   THOMAS WILSON DEFT)

   SAMUEL CLEMNY PLFT)
    VS   ) Certorari Continued as on affidavit
   JOHN McCAFFEY DEFT.) of the Defendant.

(P-140)

W. R. HERN   Plaintiff)
       VS   ) Case
JERU FERRINGTON DEFT.)

It is ordered This day came the parties by their attornies who
agree this cause be refered to Walter Carruth, Hugh Roan, Samuel Cannon,
James Cross, & James McAdow, whose decision is to be the Judgement of
the Court the referees after taking time to hear the evidence of the
parties brought into Court then awarded thus. that the suit be dismissed
by the plaintiff and that each party pay half the cost in this behalf
expended It is therefore considered by the Court that the suit be dismissed and that each party pay one half the costs.

Robert Smith a witness for the plaintiff proved two days attendance
& fifty four miles traveling &c.
     Threatt Harrison a witness   2 days
     John Hern 2 days & 54 miles traveling
     Ebenezer Hern 2 days &

POLLY JOINER   PLFT.)
     VS   ) Case
JAMES DAVIS   DEFT)

This day came the plaintiff by her attorney & prays the suit to be
dismissed and assumes all cost   It is therefore considered by the Court
that this suit be dismissed and that the Defendant recover against the
said Plaintiff their costs in this behalf expended   The costs will be
paid by James Davis   so says his attorney Foster &c.

(P-141)   PAUL SHEELY   PLFT)
          VS   ) Debt.
     RICHARD LIGGAN & CO)
              DEFT)

Argument on Demurred   This day came the parties by their attornies
and upon their argument It is considered by the Court that the demurrer
be over overruled and that the plaintiff recover against the Defendants
according to specialty amounting to one hundred and five dollars thirty
one & a fourth cents the debt in the specialty mentioned with two dollars
& five cents damages amounting in the whole to one hundred and seven
dollars and thirty six cents also his cost in this behalf expended.

ROBERT DONELSON   PLFT.) Case
       VS   ) Pleas &c.
EDMUND GREENAGE   DEFT.)

Be it remembered that heretofore to wit at March Term 1816 Edmund
Greenage was attached to answer Robert Donelson of a plea of tresspass
on the case to his damage of one hundred dollars whereupon at said
March Term 1816 the said Robert Donelson by his attorney

Harry L. Douglass, filed his decleration in the following words & figures (to wit)

STATE OF TENNESSEE)
)   March Term 1816
WILSON COUNTY   )

Robert Donelson by his attorney complains of Edmund Greenage in custody &c of a plea of tresspass on the case For the said Defendt. on the day of 181 to wit at the County aforesaid in consideration that the said plaintiff did then & there at the special instance and request of the said Defendant exchange with said Deft. a sorrel mare of the value of seventy Dollars the property of the said plaintiff for a black horse of the Defendants property he the said Defendant then & there undertook and faithfully promised said plft. that said black horse was sound and the said Plaintiff avers that confiding in the said promise and undertaking of the said Deft. did on the day and year last aforesaid exchange with said Deft. the said----- mare of the value of seventy Dollars for the said black horse, yet the said Deft (P-142) Deft not regarding his said promise & undertaking but contriving & fraudulantly intending to deceive & defraud the said plft. did not keep his said promise & undertaking so by him made as aforesaid but there by Craftily & subtily deceived & defrauded the said plft. in this to wit, that the said black horse at the time of making the said promise was not sound but on the contrary was unsound in his hind parts so much so that the said horse was and in a little time became totally useless and of no value to said plft of which the said Defet. afterwards to wit on at the County aforesaid had notice and so the said plft. is injured to the value of one hundred dollars.

Douglass atto.

Defts Pleas non assumpset statute of limitations rep. & issue

Hadlyy atto.

At June Term 1816 came the parties aforesaid by their attornies and thereupon came a jury of good and lawful men to wit Henry Howel, Josiah Chandler, John Harpole, Isham Palmer, George Tucker, Isaac Hunter, William Wilson, Richard Henderson, Carter Irby, Eli Harris, William Babb, & William Lawrence, who being elected tried and sworn the truth to speak upon the issue joined upon their oaths do say they find the Deft did assume upon himself in manner and form as the said Plaintiff in his decleration hath alledged and assess the Plaintiffs damage to sixty five Dollars. It is there fore considered by the Court that the said Plft. recover against the said defendant the said sum of sixty five Dollars as by the jury aforesaid assessed also his cost of suit in this behalf expended.

The defendant fr William Thomas a witness proved 5 days & 34 miles.
Richard Ramsey a witness 5 days

James Bradberry,   5 days
William Bradberry, 4 days
Robert Fulterton, 5 days
William Sands   3 days
Joshua Kelly   5 days
Humphrey Donelson, 3 days

from which   (P-143)   judgement the defendant prays an appeal to the next
Circuit Court to be holden for the County of Wilson at the Court house in
Lebanon on the first Monday in September next files his reasons & enters
into bond with William Anderson, & Richard Ramsey, securities whereupon
the Court grant an appeal to the next Circuit Court &c.

WILLIAM LYTLE   PLFT.)
        VS.   ) Debt.
JOHN BELL   DEFT.)

      This day came the Deft by his attorney and with the leave of the
Court withdraws his pleas heretofore plead and acknowledges the balance
of the plaintiffs Debt to be thirteen hundred & eighty seven dollars &
fifteen cents & that he justly owes the same.

      It is therefore considered by the Court that the said plaintiff
recover against the said Defendant the said sum of thirteen hundred &
eighty seven dollars & fifteen cents as by the defendant confessed also his
costs in this behalf expended & the Deft in mercy &c.

HUMPHRY CHAPPEL   PLFT.)
       VS.   ) T.A.B.
JOHN SMART   DEFT.)

JOHN SMART   PLFT.) T.A.B.
     VS.   ) Contd on Defts. appeal.
HUMPHRY CHAPPEL   DEFT.)

(P-144)

MATTHEW BROOKS   PLFT.)
     VS.   ) Case contd. on motion of the plaintiff
ELIJAH CROSS   DEFT.)

      It is ordered by the Court that a Commission issue to take the
Depo. of John Stow of Kentucky and that a notice of 20 days be given
contd.

14   THWEATT HARRISON   PLFT.)
          VS   ) Debt.
      LEONARD H. SIMS   DEFT.)

This day came the parties by their attornies and Defendant by his attorney with draws his demurer & pleas and acknowledges in the plaintiff Debt with interest amounting to three hundred and six dollars & twenty two cents & costs of suit It is therefore considered by the Court that the said plaintiff recover against the said Defendant the said sum of three hundred & six dollars and twenty two cents for his debt & interest as by the defendant confessed Also his cost of suit in this behalf expended & the deft. &c.

```
PLEASANT CRADDOCK    PLFT )
        VS                )  In Debt
RICHARD LIGGAN & CO  DEFT. )
```

This day came the parties by their attornies and thereupon came a jury of good and lawful men to wit William Stafford, William Wilson, Andrew Foster, Jehu Ferrington, John W. Lumpkin, Thomas Bonner, Josiah Stevenson, Thomas Davis, John Walker, James McFarland, William Hartsfield, & Jesse Brenson, who being elected tried and sworn the truth to speak upon the issue joined upon their oaths do say the find for the plaintiff his debt according to specialty amounting to one hundred & nineteen dollars thirty two cents, and assess the Plaintiffs damage by way of interest to three Dollars & fifty seven cents.

It is there fore considered by the Court that the said plaintiff recover against the said Defendants the said sum of one hundred & nineteen Dollars for his debt also three dollars fifty seven cents damages as by the jury aforesaid assessed also his cost in this behalf expended &c.

```
(P-145)  JAMES HENDERSON  PLFT. )
              VS                )  Case
         ARMSTEAD LANE     DEFT. )
```

This day came the parties by their attornies also a jury of good and lawful men to wit George Tucker, John Harpole, Charles Luck, Josiah Chandler, William Laurence, Richard Henderson, William Babb, Andrew Foster, Carter Irby, Eli Harris, Jeremiah Brown, & William Stafford, who being elected tried and sworn upon their oaths do say the find for the plaintiff and assess his damage to one cent It is therefore considered by the Court that the Plaintiff recover against the said Defendant one cent as by the jury assessed also his cost of suit &c.

```
JAMES ROANE       PLFT.   )
        VS                )  Debt
B. TATUM & OTHERS  DEFT.  )
```

This day came the parties by their attornies also a jury of good and lawful men to wit William Stafford, William Wilson, Andrew Foster, Jehu Ferrington, John W. Lumpkin, Thomas Bonner, Josiah Stephenson, Thomas Davis, John Walker, James McFarlin, William Hartsfield, and Jesse Brenson, who being elected tried and sworn the truth to speak upon the issue joined upon their oaths do say they find the Defendants has not paid the debt in the plaintiffs decleration mentioned amounting eighty five Dollars and assess the damages occasioned by the detention of said debt to four dollars

& sixty seven and a half cents.

It is therefore considered by the Court that the said plaintiff recover against the said Defts. the said sum of eighty five dollars for his debt, also four dollars sixty seven and a half cents.

~~It is therefore considered by the Court that the said plaintiff recover against the said Defts. the said sum of eighty five dollars for his debt, also four dollars sixty seven and a half cents~~ the damages aforesaid by the jury aforesaid assessed also his cost in this behalf expended &c.

(P-146)

PORTER & DALE	PLFT.	)
VS		) Case
BENJAMIN MOTLEY	DEFT.	)

This day came the parties by their attornies & also a jury of good and lawful men to wit ~~who being elected tried and sworn the truth to speak upon the issue joined upon their oaths~~ Henry Howel, Josiah Chandler, John Harpole, Isham Palmer, George Tucker, Isaac Hunter, William Wilson, Richard Henderson, Carter Irby, Eli Harris William Babb, & William Laurence, who being elected tried and sworn the truth to speak upon the issue joined upon their oaths do say the find the pleas in favour of the plaintiffs and that the said Defendant has not paid the debt in the plaintiffs decleration mentioned amounting to - and hundred dollars and assess his damages for the detention of said debt to three dollars, It is therefore considered by the Court that the said plaintiff recover against the said Deft. the said sum of one hundred dollars for his debt also three dollars the damages aforesaid ~~his~~ by the jurors aforesaid assessed also his costs in that behalf expended &c.

ADAM MIRES	PLFT.	) T.A.B.
VS		)
THOMAS C. DAVIS	DEFT.	)

The plaintiff by his attorney comes into Court and says he is unwilling any further to prosecute his said suit & prays the same to be dismissed

The Defendant at the same - Comes into Court and assumes all cost. It is therefore ordered by the court that this suit be dismissed and that the Plaintiff recover against the Defendant all the cost in this behalf expended & the deft. &c.

READ & WASHINGTON	PLFT.	)
VS.		) Case
BAKER RATHER & WIFE	DEFT.	)

Pleas &c.

Be it remembered that heretofore to wit At March term 1816 Baker Rather & Sarah G. Rather was attached to answer Thomas J. Read and Gilbert

C. Washington merchants and partners in trade, trading under the firm of Read & Washington in a plea of (P-147) tresspass on the Case to their damage one hundred dollars.

Whereupon at said March Term 1816 the said Read and Washington, by Samuel Anderson Esqrs their attorney & filed their decleration in the following words and figures (to wit)

STATE OF TENNESSEE)
) March Sessions 1816
WILSON COUNTY   )

Thomas J. Read, & Gilbert G. Washington merchants and partners in trade trading under the firm of Read and Washington by their attorney complains of Baker Rather & Sarah G. his wife in custody & in a plea of tresspass on the case for that whereas the said Sarah G. while Sale on the____ day of_____ in the County aforesaid was indebted to the said plaintiff in the sum of sixty one ___ seventy five cents, for goods wares and merchandise before that time sold and delivered to the said Sarah G. at her special instance and request for money before that time laid out and expended for the use of the said Sarah G. at her like special instance & request and for money before that time but and accomodated by said Plaintiff to the said Sarah G. at her like special instance and request in consideration whereof the said Plaintiff (to wit) on the same day and year aforesaid to wit in the County aforesaid undertook and faithfully promised to pay said sum of money when she should thereto afterwards requested nevertheless the said Sarah G. while sole and the said Baker Rather and Sarah G. his wife since their intermarriage hath not paid said sum of money or any part thereof altho often requested at, (to wit) in the County aforesaid on the same day and year aforesaid But to pay the same hath hither to wholly refused and still doth refuse, the same to pay or any part thereof to the damage of the Plaintiff one hundred dollars, whereupon he sues & pledges to Prosecute –

S. Anderson atty.

The Defendants pleas nonassumpset & issue, and for further plea in this behalf said defendant (P-148) say the said Read and Washington before and at the time of Commencement of this suit at Nashville to wit at the County of Wilson aforesaid was and still are indebted to the said Defendants in a large sum of money (to wit) the sum of one hundred and sixty six dollars for boarding Gilbert G. Washington one of the firm of Read & Washington by the said Sarah G. before the intermarriage with the said Baker, nine months and keeping and feeding the horses of the said Read & Washington nine months ____ which said sum of money so due, lawing from the said Read & Washington, to the said Defendants as, aforesaid exceeds the damages & interest by the said Read and Washington, by the reason of the non performance by the said Defendants of the said several supposed promises and undertaking in the said Decleration mentioned and out of which said sum of monies so due and oweing from the said Plaintiff to the said defendants they the said Defts are ready and willing to sett off and allow to the said plaintiff the full amount of the said damages according to the firm of the Statute made & provided and the said Defendants are ready to verify - wherefore they pray judgement of the said plaintiffs their action there of against them to have and maintain &c.

Douglass atto.
for Defendants

Replecation issue .
Anderson attorney for Plaintiff
Douglass atto for Defendants Contd.

At June Term 1816 came the parties aforesaid & for further plead the said Baker who then comes & says that the said Read & Washington ought not further to maintain their said action against him the said Baker because he says that since the last continuance of the plea between them, the said Read & Washington & the said (P-149) Baker Wrather and wife Sarah G. Wrather, to wit after March term 1816 from which day the said parties were last continued hereto the present term (to wit) June Term 1816 on the 31st day of May in the year 1816 at Lebanon in the County of Wilson the said Sarah G. Wrather, one of the defendants in this action and wife of the said Baker Wrather died and this he is ready to verify wherefore said Baker Wrather prays judgement if the said Read & Washington ought further to maintain their action thereof against him

Baker Wrather
Wilson County Leb.

Baker Wrather appeared in open Court and made oath that the facts stated in the above plea are true.

Test. John Allcorn, Clk.
Demurrer to the above plea.
S. Anderson atty. for Plaintiff

Joinder in Demurred
H. L. Douglass att.

And now at this term to wit June term 1811 came the parties by their attornies and there upon on argument of the plaintiff demurrer to the plea of the defendant last above pleaded it is considered by the Court that the said demurrer be overuled and that said defendant go hence without day and recover of said plaintiff his cost by him above his defence in this behalf expended.

(P-150)   EDMUND CRUTCHER   PLFT.)
             VS.   ) In Debt.
         WALLACE CALDWELL   DEFT.)

This day came the parties by their Attornies and thereupon argument being had before the Court, It is considered by the Court that the plea of infamy by the Defendant pleaded is good and sufficient in law and that the Defendant go hence without day - and recover against the said Plaintiff his cost in this behalf expended &c.

JOHN A EATON   PLFT.)
     VS.   ) In Debt.
THOMAS DAVIS & OTHERS DEFTS)

This day came the parties by their attornies, The Defendant withdraws his plea in abatement and acknowledges the plaintiffs action for of one hundred and fifty dollars for his debt and and four dollars and twenty five cents for damages amounting in the whole to one hundred & fifty four dollars and twenty five cents, It is therefore considered by the Court that the said plaintiff recover against the said defendants the said sum of one hundred and fifty four dollars and twenty five cents for his Debt and damages as by the defendant confessed also his cost in this behalf expended.

DAVID ENOCHS   PLFT.)
     VS   ) Tresspass
CARTER CRUTCHER   DEFT.)

Contd. on affidavit of the Plft.

PHEBY PHILLIPS   PLFT.)
     VS.   ) Tresspass
CARTER CRUTCHER   DEFT.)

Contd on affidavit of the Plft.

SAMUEL HOGG   PLFT.)
     VS.   ) Indict
LEONARD H. SIMMS   DEFT.)

Dismissed by the Plft.   Deft. assumes the cost

(P-151)

EDMUND CRUTCHER   PLFT.)
     VS.   ) In Debt
JNO M. LUMKIN   DEFT.)

Pleas point and issue. This day came the parties by their attornies and the defendant agrees to with draw his plea and acknowledges the Plfts action for five hundred and three dollars & fifty cents his debt and Interest thereon.

It is therefore considered by the Court that the said plaintiff recover against the said Defendant the sum of five hundred and three dollars & fifty cents for his Debt also __ Damages by way of interest as by the defendant confessed & also his cost about his suit in this behalf expended.

JOSEPH TURNHAM   PLFT.)
     VS   )   Case contd. under former rule.
JOHN W. NICHOLS   DEFT.)

ELI   ANDERSON   PLFT.)   Case
      VS.   )   Slander
SAML ALLEN & WIFE DEFTS)

This day came the parties by their attornies, and thereupon came a
jury of good and lawful men (to wit) Jeremiah Brown, Charles Lock, Andrew
Foster, John Ferrington, William Stafford, George Wynne, Robert Donelson,
William Sands, Beverly Williams, James Wilkerson, Samuel W. Sherrill, &
Robert Fullerton, who being elected tried and sworn the truth to speak
upon the issue joined upon their oaths do say they Defendants are not
guilty ~~in in pleading they may alledged~~ of speaking the slanderous words
in manner and form as the plaintiff against them hath declared as the said
Defendant in pleading hath elledged

It is there fore considered by the Court that the Plaintiff take nothing, and that the Defendant go hence without day and recover against the
said Plaintiff the cost by him about (P-152)   about his defence in this
behalf expended &c.

    William Anderson & wife proved 2 days each
    Ransom Gwyn Esqr. proved 5 days
    John Bowenan proved 3 days
    Eddings Chandler, proved four days
    Baily Chandler proved three days
    James Shaw, proved five days
    Cathanne Shaw proved 4 days
    William Chandler proved four days
    Lephiniah Neil proved five days
    Lephiniah Neil Sen. proved five days

    Pleas &c.

MOODY P. HAYNES   PLFT.)
     VS.   )   Case
JEREMIAH FLETCHER DEFT.)

Be it remembered that hereto fore to wit at March Session 1816
Jeremiah Fletcher, was attached to answer Moody P. Hayns of a plea of
tresspass on the case to his damage two hundred dollars where upon at
said March Term 1816 the said Moody P. Heynes by his attorney Harry L.
Douglass, esquire filed his decleration in the following words and figures
(to wit)

STATE OF TENNESSEE) March
WILSON COUNTY LEB.   ) Session 1816

Moody P. Hayns by his attorney complains of Jeremiah Fletcher, in custody &c of a plea of tresspass on the case, For that according to the law and custom of the land the Inn keepers who keep common Inns to lodge travelers therein who abide in the same are bound to keep their goods and Chattels being within those Inns day and night with out notice pilfering or loss so that no ~~danger loss~~ (P-153) danger or loss might happen to any such travellers or guest, for want of care in such innkeepers or their servants, and whereas on the __ day of December in the year 1815 the said Jeremiah Fletcher, was keeping a common Inn having a Sign (to wit) in the County of Wilson aforesaid the said Moody P. Hayns, having certain goods (to wit) one broad-clothe - coat of the value of thirty five Dollars & one vest of the value of seven dollars one other vest of the value of five dollars one pair pantaloons of the value of fifteen dollars, one pair of boots of the value of twelve dollars, one pair gloves of the value of one dollar, one note for ninety five dollars and three dollars in silver as his guest in the same Inn. But certain malefactory on the   day of aforesaid the goods aforesaid of the said Plaintiff being in the Inn aforesaid of the said Jeremiah Fletcher, at the County aforesaid from and by the negligence of the said Jeremiah Fletcher being in the possession of the goods aforesaid took carried away and converted to their own use and other wrongs to him did against the peace &c &c to the damage of &c.

                                        Douglass, atto.

And the defendant by his attorney says he is not guilty in manner and form as the Plaintiff in declaring against him hath alledged and of this he puts himself upon the County &c

                          S. Anderson   attoy.

Pleas filed   Rule Plead &try &c.

Now at June Term 1816 came the parties by their attornies and also a jury of good and lawful men to wit Henry Howel, Josiah Chandler, John Harpole, Isham Palmer, George Tucker, Isaac Hunter, William Wilson, Richard Henderson, Carter Irby, Eli. Harris, William Babb, & William Lawrence, who being elected tried and sworn the truth to speak upon the issue joined upon their oaths do say the defendants is guilty as the plaintiff in his decleration hath alledged and assess the plaintiff damages to sixty (P-154) sixty five dollars & fifty cents. It is there fore considered by the Court that the said Plaintiff recover against the said Defendant the said sum of sixty five Dollars and fifty cents the damages aforesaid by the jury aforesaid assessed ~~also~~ also his cost of suit in this behalf expended &c.

From which judgement the said Defendant prays an appeal to the ensuing Circuit Court to be holden for the County of Wilson at the Court house in Lebanon on the first Monday in September next upon the Defendants entering into bond with Obediah Spradling, his security & reasons filed by his attorney It is the opinion of the Court that an appeal be granted to the next Circuit Court &c.

WILSON & MEREDITH PLFT.   )
       VS.   ) Appeal
SALLY WILLIAMS & T.BONNER)
          DEFTS.   )

This day came the parties by their attornies and also a jury of good and lawful men to wit Wm Lawrence, Jeremiah Brown, George Wynne, William Stafford, William Wilson, Joseph Cole, Frances Palmer James Word, William Rickets, John Fisher, Samuel W. Sherrell, and Eli Edwards, who being elected tried and sworn the truth to speak upon their oaths do say the find for the Defendants, It is therefore considered by the Court that the said Defendants go hence without day & recover against the plaintiff the cost about his defence in this behalf expended &c.

(P-155)

SAMPSON ORGAN   PLFT.   )
     VS.   ) Attachment.
SOLOMAN WILLIAMS DEFT.   )

This day came the plaintiff and filed his decleration in the words & figures to wit Wilson } Leb. Term 1816 Simpson Organ by his attorney complains of Soloman Williams whoes property has been attached & of a plea that he render to him the sum of two hundred and fifty dollars which to him he owes and from him unjustly detains for that where as the said Soloman on the 27th day of November 1815 at   in the County aforesaid made his certain bill single, here produced to the Court and there by promised to pay the said Simpson on or before the first day of April, then next the sum of one hundred & two Dollars and on the sixth day of November 1815 said Defendant made his bill single here produced in Court & thereby promised to pay said plaintiff on or before the first day of April then next, the sum of sixty dollars at ___ in the County aforesaid and on the 27th day of November 1815 said Defendant made his bill single here produced to the Court and there by promised to pay said plaintiff sixty dollars on or before the first day of April then next at the County aforesaid and on the 27th day of November 1815 at in the County aforesaid said defendant made his bill single here produced to the Court and thereby promised to pay the said plaintiff on or before the first day of April then next ensuing the sum of eleven dollars at __ in the County aforesaid nevertheless tho requested hath not paid the said several bills single on the day of payment or at any time before or since to plaintiffs damage two hundred and fifty dollars and therefore he has brought suit &c. Decleration filed the 3d day of the term.

Will Williams J.P.

And thereupon upon on the fifth day of said June Term 1816, The Defendant being solemnly called and came not nor is any defence made It is therefore considered by the Court that Judgement by default find according to the specialty filed balance of Debt amounting to two hundred and twenty eight (P-156) dollars ninety six & a half cents damages by way of interest to three dollars & five cents & costs of suit in this behalf. It is further ordered by the Court that their property attached be sold to satisfy said debt and cost &c.

```
JOHN LAY        PLFT.    )
   VS.                   ) Attachment
SOLOMAN WILLIAMS DEFT.   )
```

The Defendant Soleman Williams, being solemnly called & came not and it appearing on the attachment no property found But that William Stanly & Arthur Hankins, are summoned by a garnashee warrant to say upon oath what they are indebted to the said Soloman Williams & the notes filed by the plaintiff for the sum of one hundred and twenty three dollars.

Arthur Hankins on his garnishee upon oath says his indebted eight Dollars eighty cents on motion of the Plaintiff attorney It is considered by the court that Judgement final be rendered against the said Defendant and that the said Plaintiff recover against the said defendant the sum of one hundred and twenty three dollars for his debt also two dollars interest thereon and also his cost of suit in this behalf expended.

It is further considered by the Court that the said Plaintiff recover against Arthur Hankins, the sum of eight Dollars & eighty Cents in part of the said Judgement against the defendant (P-157)

```
EDMUND CRUTCHER    PLFT )
   VS.                  )
JEHU FERRINGTON,   DEFT. )
```

On this 21st day of June 1816 the Defendant Jehu Ferrington, came into Court and acknowledges himself indebted to the said Edmund Crutcher, the sum of three hundred Dollars with interest thereon from the 25th December 1815 amounting to eight Dollars and seventy five cents

It is thereupon considered by the Court that Judgement be rendered against the said Defendant Jehu for the said sum of three hundred & eight Dollars and and seventy five cents the amount of said Debt and interest due thereon up to this date. Also the Cost of this Judgement Confessed and that the said Plaintiff have his execution &c.

(P-158) Records of September Term 1816 at a Court of pleas &c began &c.

JOHN NICHOLS   PLFT.   )
   VS.   ) In Debt.
ABNER WASSON   DEFT.   )

This day came the plaintiff by his attorney and the said defendant in proper person & there upon with leave of the Court withdraws his plea to the decleration filed by plaintiff in this action & acknowledges the debt in plaintiffs decleration mentioned with interest thereon amounting in the whole to two hundred & one dollars sixty two & a half cents. It is therefore considered by the Court that the said plaintiff recover of said defendant the said sum of two hundred & one dollars sixty two & a half cents & also his cost by him about his suit in this behalf expended &c.

BENJAMIN GRAVES   )
   VS.   ) Motion on an Execution.
EDMUND FLETCHER)

(P-159) Pleas before the Court of pleas & quarter sessions began and held for the County of Wilson at the Court house or place of holding Court on Monday the 16th day of September 1816 & 41st year of Am. Independence

BENTON MODGLIN   PLFT.   )
   VS.   ) Appeal
JESSE RODES   DEFT.   )

STATE OF TENNESSEE)
WILSON COUNTY   )
) To any lawful officer to execute sumon Jesse Rhodes to appear before me or some other justice of the peace for said County to answer the complaint of Benton Modglin, in a plea of debt due by account sum under one hundred dollars

Given under my hand the 1st July 1816.

Edward Harris   J.P.

Executed by William Sypert, Const.

Judgement rendered against the defendant for seven dollars & fifty cents & costs of suit – from which judgement the defendant prays an appeal to the Court of pleas & quarter sessions for the County of Wilson which is granted, he having given Daniel Richmond security according to law July 6th 1816

Jas. Johnson, J.P.

and now at this term to wit September Term 1816 Came the parties aforesaid by their attornies – on motion of the plaintiffs attorney to dismiss the appeal and after argument before the Court & the motion by them fully understood, It is considered by the Court that the motion aforesaid be sustained and that the appeal be dismissed & that the Judgement of the Justice øf ţhµ be affirmed and that the Plaintiff recover against the Defendant the said sum of seven dollars & fifty cents – also the costs on this behalf (P-160) expended.

From which judgement the Defendant prays an appeal to the next Circuit Court
to be holden for the County of Wilson at the Court house in the town of Lebanon on the first Monday in March next The defendant intering into bond as the
law directs with Samuel Anderson, and Daniel Richmond, his securities & the
attorney for the Defendant filing reasons for the appeal It is considered by
the Court that an appeal be granted.

        Bill of Costs.
            Constable Sypert Executing warrant DC. $ .50
            Judgement & law tax   16.25
            Copy record & seal   1.40
            Attorney Foster   1.25
                          - - - - - - - - - -

JOHN NICHOLS   PLFT.)
    VS.   ) Debt.
ABNER WASON   DEFT)

(P-161)
            Records of September Term 1816

(P-162)   at a Court of pleas and quarter sessions began & held for the
County of Wilson at the Courthouse in Lebanon on Monday the 17th day of
March 1916 and 41st year of American Independence

MATTHEW BROOKS   PLAINTIFF)
    VS.   ) In Case
ELIJAH CROSS   DEFENDANT)

     Be it remembered that heretofore at March Term 1816 Elijah Cross was
attached to answer Matthew Brooks in a plea of tresspass on the case to his
damage three hundred dollars whereupon at said March Term the said Matthew
Brooks by his attorney Saml. Anderson Esquire filed his declaration in
the following words and figures (to wit)

STATE OF TENNESSEE)
WILSON COUNTY   ) March sessions 1816

     Matthew Brooks by his attorney complains of Elijah Cross in Custody of
the sheriff &c in a plea of tresspass on the case for that whereas the said
plaintiff on the __ day of ____ to wit in the County aforesaid was possessed
of a certain Sorrel horse rising 7 years old of the value of one hundred
dollars as of his own property and being there of possessed said plaintiff
afterwards to wit on the same day and year aforesaid in the County aforesaid
Came Casually lost the same, which same horse afterwards on the same day
and year aforesaid came into the hands & possession of the said Defendant
by finding nevertheless said Defendant well knowing the said sorrel horse
to be the property of the said plaintiff and of right belonged to him But
contriving & fraudulently intending craftily subtily to deceive and defraud

the plaintiff in this behalf hath not yet delivered said sorrel horse to the plaintiff altho he hath been thereto often requested, Requested on the same day and year aforesaid in the County aforesaid But the Defendant afterwards to wit on the same day and year aforesaid to wit in the County aforesaid converted and exposed the said (P-163) Sorrel horse to his own use to the damage of the plaintiff three hundred dollars wherefore he sues and pledges to prosecute.

S. Anderson atto.

At said March Term aforesaid the defendant by his attorney pleas not guilty leave to plead specially so as not to delay the trial replication & issue.

From said March Term 1816 this cause was continued until March Term 1817 whereupon Came the parties by their attornies and also a jury of good & lawful men (to wit) William New, William Hardin George Harpole, Thomas Dill, Clement Johnson, Edward Clay, Josiah Smith, Elijah Truitt, Beverly Williams, John W. Nichols, Carter Irby, & Thomas S. Green, who being elected tried and sworn the truth to speak upon the issue joined upon their oaths do say the Defendant is not guilty in manner & form as the plaintiff against hath Complained, It is therefore considered by the Court that the defendant go hence without day and recover against the said plaintiff his cost of suit in this behalf expended. From which judgement the plaintiff prays an appeal to the next ensuing Circuit Court to be holden for the County of Wilson at the Court house in the town of Lebanon on the first Monday in September next and upon entering into bond as the law directs and filing reasons an appeal is granted by the Court &c.

Bill of Cost to wit Clerks fee writ law tax and prosecution
bond   20.2½
Issuing 4 subpoenas at 20 cts each   80.00
3 Continances at 40 cts each   1.20
Judgement & record - - - - - - - - - - - -   1.00
Transcript of record & seal   140 - - - - - - - - - -   1 40
            Sheriff fees.
Executing writ & taking bond   1 25- - - - - - -   1 25
Executing five subpoenas 25 cts each   1 25
Attorney Douglass   _2 50_
                                                             11.42½

(P-164)   Pleas before the Court of pleas & quarter sessions began and held for the County of Wilson at the Court house in Lebanon , on Monday the seventeenth of March 1817 and of the independence of the United States the forty first.

JACOB THOMPSON   PLFT.   )
     VS.   )   In Debt.
FREEMAN MODGLIN B. MODGLIN &   )
HIGDON HARRINGTON   DEFTS.   )

Be it remembered that here to fore (to wit) on the nineteenth day of February 1817 Truman Modglin B. Modglin, & Higdon Harrington was attached to ans. Jacob Thompson, in a plea that they render unto him one hundred and ninety one dollars & fifty five cents which they owe to him & from him unjustly detains to his damage fifty dollars.

Whereupon the said Jacob Thompson by Harry Cage, esquire his attorney came into Court of said March Term 1817 and filed his declaration in the following words and figures (to wit)

STATE OF TENNESSEE   WILSON COUNTY COURT   March Term 1817

Jacob Thompson by his atto. complains of Truman Modglin B. Modglin & Higdon Harrington in custody &c of a plea that they render unto him one hundred and ninety dollars & fifty five cents which they owe to him & from him unjustly detains. For that whereas the said Truman Modglin, B. Modglin & Higdon Harrington Defendants on the 21st day of March 1816 in the County aforesaid by their writing obligatory of that date sealed with their own proper seals and here in Court to be produced bound and acknowledged themselves to be indebted to the plaintiff in the sum of one hundred & ninety one dollars & fifty five cents to be paid to the plaintiff one day after date yet though often requested the said Defendants have never paid the same to the plaintiff nor to any other person to his use, but the same have wholly refused to pay to the damage of the plaintiff fifty dollars and thereupon he bring suit

Cage   atto.

At said March Term 1817 the defendant pleads payment set off replication & issue —

(P-165)   From March Term this suit is continued until September Term 1817 and thereupon came the parties aforesaid by their attornies, also a jury of good and lawful men (to wit) Joshua Bradberry, Morris Hallum, Samuel Gray, William Neil, William Marshall, Sterling Tarpley, William Telford, Gideon Alexander, David McMurry, John Brennon, William Jones, & George McWhirter who being elected tried and sworn the truth to speak upon the issue joined upon their oaths do say the defendants have not paid the debt in the plaintiffs declaration mentioned as in pleading he hath alledged and assess his damage to sixteen dollars & seventy five cents —

It is thereupon considered by the Court that the said plaintiff recover against the said Defendand one hundred and ninety dollars & fifty five cents for his Debt. also sixteen dollars seventy five cents for his damages as by the jurors aforesaid assessed.

Also his cost of suit in this behalf expended from which judgement the plaintiff prays an appeal to the next Circuit Court to be holden for the County of Wilson at the Court house in Lebanon on the first Monday in March next Entered into bond filed reasons &c and there upon an appeal is granted &c.

Bill of Cost.

Clerks fee
    writ law tax & prosecuting bond   20.¼
    Judgement & record - - -   1 00
    Copy record & seal   1 40
Sheriff fees Three arrest and one bond   3 25
Calling Cause and jury   16
Attorney Harry Cage $10.13½

(P-166)   Pleas before the Court of pleas & quarter sessions began and held
for the County of Wilson at the Court house in the town of Lebanon on the
third Monday in September 1817 and of the Independence of the United States
the forty first.

THOMAS EASTLAND   PLFT.   )
    VS.   ) In Debt
JOSEPH T. WILLIAMS DEFT.)

Be it remembered that heretofore (to wit) on the third Monday in June
1817 Joseph T. Williams was attached to answer Thomas Eastland in a plea
that he render unto him one hundred & fifty dollars which he owes to him &
from him unjustly detains to his damage fifty dollars.

Whereupon the said Thomas Eastland by New Hadly, esquire his attorney,
came into Court of said June Term 1817 and filed his decleration in the
following words and figures (to wit)

STATE OF TENNESSEE   WILSON COUNTY COURT June Term 1817

Thomas Eastland by his attorney complains of Joseph T. Williams in
custody &c in a plea that he render to him one hundred and fifty dollars
which to him he owes and from him unjustly detains For that whereas the
said Joseph T. Williams by his certain writing obligatory made at the County
aforesaid on the 31st day of December 1815 sealed with the seal of the said
Joseph T. Williams, and to the Court now shewn the date whereof is the same
day and year last aforesaid bound himself & promised to pay Thomas Eastland
the plaintiff the said sum of one hundred and fifty dollars for value recd.
six months after the date of said writing obligatory nevertheless the said
defendant tho often requested hath not paid said one hundred & fifty dollars
but the same and every part thereof to pay hath refused & still refuses to
the damage of the said plaintiff fifty dollars and therefore he sues &c.

                                      Hadly   atto.
at said June Term 1817

The defendant pleads payment set off replication & issue

(P-167) From said June Term this suit is continued until September Term
1817 and thereupon Came the parties aforesaid by their attornies also a

jury of good and lawful men (to wit) Joshua Bradberry, Morris Mellum, Saml. Gray Wm Neil, Wm Marshall, Sterling Tarpley, Wm. Telford, Gideon Alexander David McMurry, John Drennon, William Jones, & George McWhirter, who being elected tried and sworn the truth to speak upon the issue joined upon their oths do say they find the defendant has not paid the debt in the specialty mentioned of one hundred and fifty dollars and assess the plaintiffs damages by reason of the detention thereof to eleven dollars and twenty five cents.

It is therefore considered by the Court that said plaintiff recover of said defendant the debt and damages aforesaid by the jury aforesaid in form aforesaid assessed amounting to one hundred & sixty one dollars and twenty five cents and also his Costs by him about his suit in this behalf expended and that Deft &c -

From which judgement the defendant prays an appeal to the next Circuit Court to be holden for the county of Wilson at the Court house in Lebanon on the first Monday in March next entered into bond filed reasons &c and thereupon an appeal is granted.

Bill of Costs

Clerks fees

Writ lane tax & bond	$202½
Judgement & record & alias writ	140
Copy record and Seal	140

Sheriff fees.

Arrest & bond	125
Calling Cause & jury	16
Attorney Wm. Hadly	250
	$ 853½

(P-168) Pleas before the Court of pleas and quarter sessions began and held for the county of Wilson at the Court house in Lebanon on Monday the 17th day of March 1817 & 41st year of our Independence.

JOHN SMART   PLFT.   )
    VS.   ) Appeal
SMITH HANSBRO   DEFT.   )

Be it remembered that at said March Term 1817 Edward Harris esquire filed in court on the first day of the Term papers in the following words and figures (to wit)

STATE OF TENNESSEE   )
WILSON COUNTY   )
) To any lawful officer to execute summons Smith Hansbro to appear before me or some other justice of the peace for said County to answer John Smart in a plea of debt due by account under fifty dollars under a warrant given under my hand this 15th day of February 1817

                        Jas. Johnson   J.P.

Trial posponed until February 24th 1817 February 24 1817 Judgement entered against the defendant for $40. given under my hand.

                                    Edward Harris J.P.
From which Judgement the defendant appeals to the County Court & give bond
& security.

                                    Edward Harris J.P.

From which term this suit stands continued from term to term until
September Term 1817.

At which term came the parties by their attornies and also a jury of
good and lawful men (to wit) Joshua Bradberry, Morris Hallum, Saml. Gray,
Wm. Neil, Wm. Marshall, William Donnell, Wm. Telford, Gideon Alexander,
David McMurry, John Drennon, William Jones, & George McWhirter who being
elected tried and sworn the truth to speak upon the trial of this cause upon their oaths do say they find for the plaintiff ten dollars

It is therefore considered by the Court that (P-169)   the plaintiff
recover against the defendant the sum of ten dollars as by the Jurors aforesaid*also his costs of suit in this behalf expended.

From which judgement the plaintiff prays an appeal to the next Circuit
Court to be holden for the County of Wilson at the Court house in Lebanon
on the first Monday in March next entered into bond as the law directs filed
reasons &c upon which it is ordered by the Court that an appeal be granted

        Bill of Costs.

Constable executing warrant ...	$	50
Law tax 62½ cents		62½
one continuance 40		
3 Subpoenas 60 cts		1.00
Judgement 100 cts		1.00
Copy record 60 cts appeal bond 60 cts		
Seal 80 - --- -		2.00
Sheriff executing 7 subpoenas at 25 cts		
each		1.75
Calling cause and jury		16
Attorney E. H. Foster		1.25
Edward Harris a witness		1.50
William Allen a witness		6.00
William Sypert a witness		2.00
		17 78½

(P-170)

Pleas before the court of pleas and quarter sessions began and held for
the County of Wilson at Lebanon on Monday the fifteenth day of September
1817 and in the 41st year of our Independence.

JOHN DONELSON   PLFT.)
      VS.   ) In Debt
RICHARD DRAKE   DEFT.)

* in form aforesaid assessed

Be it remembered that heretofore to wit, on the third Monday of September 1817 Richard Drake was attached to answer John Donelson of a plea that he render unto him three hundred & ten dollars which to him he owes and from him unjustly detains to his damage one hundred and fifty dollars.

Whereupon the said John Donelson by his attorney Harry Cage Esquire Came into Court at said September Term 1817 and filed his bond in the following words and figures (to wit) on or before the twenty fifth day of December eighteen hundred and fourteen I promise to pay unto John Donelson, the just and full sum of three hundred & ten dollars, but is to pay interest on the above sum from the twenty fifth day of February next ensuing. It being for value recd. As witness my hand and seal this 1st day of December 1813

Richard Drake

Test Jeremiah Smith.

To which bond the defendant by his attorney E. H. Foster esquire pleads payment setoff replication & issue.

At December Term 1817 Came the parties aforesaid by their attornies and aforesaid and also a jury of good and lawful men (to wit) Benjamin Davidson, James Stone, Coleman Stone, Thomas Green, John Hern, Higdon Harrington, Simpson Organ, Peter Calling, Thomas Byrn, William McHaney, William Bonner, & Joseph Lester, who being elected tried and sworn the truth to speak upon the issue joined upon their oaths do say the defendant hath not paid to the plaintiff the sum of three hundred & ten dollars the amount expended in his bond filed (P-171) and assess the damage of the plaintiff to seventy dollars and seventy eight cents.

It is therefore considered by the Court that the plaintiff recover against the defendant the sum of three hundred and ten dollars for his debt, also seventy dollars seventy eight cents for his damages. as by the jurors aforesaid, inform aforesaid assessed amounting in the whole to three hundred and eighty dollars seventy eight cents, also his costs of suit in this behalf expended.

From which judgement the said defendant prays an appeal to the next Circuit Court to be holden for the County of Wilson at the Court house in Lebanon on the first Monday in March next who entered into bond as the law directs with Britton Drake his security filed reasons &c whereupon an appeal is granted &c.

Bill of Costs &c

Writ Law tax & prosecution bond	$202½
Judgement 100 cts appeal bond 60 cts	160
Transcript of record & seal	140
Sheriff arrest & bond calling court & Jury	141
Attorney Cage	2 50
	8.93½

(P-172)   Pleas before the Court of pleas and quarter sessions began and
held for the County of Wilson at the Court house in Lebanon on the third
Monday in June 1817 and 41st year of our Independence.

JOHN P. SLAUGHTER & SARAH HIS WIFE.   PLFT.   )
                VS.   ) Appeal
WILLIAM CLIFTON   DEFT.   )

STATE OF TENNESSEE   )
WILSON COUNTY   )   To any lawful officer execute & return Summon.

William Clifton to appear before me on some other justice of the peace
for said County to answer the complaints of John P. Slaughter and Sarah
his wife in a plea of debt due by account a sum under a warrant given under
my hand and seal this 19th March 1817.

                              Isham F. Davis, J.P.

Summon Jehu Ferrington for the Plft. & Coleman Stone & Benjamin T. Motly,
for the defendant Edward Harris J.P.
Executed by John B. Turnham constable March 21st 1817

     Judgement granted against the defendant for thirty dollars & cost of
suit.
                         H. Shelby   J.P.
     An appeal prayed and granted by giving Benjamin T. Motley security.

                         H. Shelby   J.P.

     From which Term last aforesaid (to wit) June Term 1817 this cause
stands continued until December Term 1817 at which term came the parties
by their attornies and also a jury of good and lawful men (to wit) John
Cartwright, Franklin Foster, Thomas Cartwright, Thomas Davis, George
Pyrtle, Benjamin Alexander, Alex Marrs, Nathan Sparks, John Clemmons,
John Phillips, Daniel Small, & Jacob Thomas who being elected tried and
sworn the truth to speak upon the trial of this cause upon their oaths
do say they find for the Defendant.

(P-173)   It is therefore considered by the Court that the said defendant
go hence without day & recover against the said John P. Slaughter, &
Sarah his wife the cost in this behalf expended. From which judgement
the plaintiff prayed and obtained an appeal to the next Circuit Court to
be holden at the Court house in Lebanon on the third Monday in March next.
entered into bond as the law directs filed reasons &c.

     Bill of Costs
     Constable executing warrant $ .50
     1 continuance 40 cts Law tax 62½   1 02½
     Judgement 100. Appeal bond 60
          Copy record   2 20

Transcript and Seal	80 cts	
3 spas. 60		5.12½
Sheriff executing 4 subpoenas		100
Calling cause and jury		16
Attorney E. H. Foster		125
John B. Turnham a witness		350
Coleman Stone a witness		150
Benjamin T. Motley a witness		4.00
		$ 16.53½

(P-174)   Pleas before the Court of pleas and quarter sessions began and held for the county of Wilson at the Court house in the town of Lebanon on the third Monday in March 1817 and forty first year of our Independence

WILLIAM MADDOX   PLFT.)
    VS.   ) In Trover
PHILIP JOHNSON   DEFT.)

Be it remembered that heretofore to wit on the third Monday in March 1817 Philip Johnson was attached to answer William Maddox in a plea of tresspass the case in trover to his damage one hundred & fifty dollars.

At said March Term 1817 the rule of Court was thus - time to declare so as not to delay the trial whereupon at June Term 1817 came the said plfts. by his attorney E. H. Foster esquire & filed his declaration in the following words and figures to wit

STATE OF TENNESSEE WILSON COUNTY JUNE TERM 1817 William Maddox by his atto. complains of Phillip Johnson in Custody &c in a plea of tresspass on the case for that wheras the said Plft. heretofore to wit on the day of   in the year of   at Lebanon in the County aforesaid was possessed of a certain still and still cap thereto appertaining as of his own proper goods and chattels of great value to wit of the value of $100 and being so possessed these of the said Plain afterwards to wit on the day of   in the year aforesaid at Lebanon aforesaid casually lost the said still & still cap thereto appertaining, out of his possession and the same afterwards to wit on the day and year last aforesaid mentioned at the place aforesaid Came into the possession of the sd. Deft. by finding the same yet the said Deft. well knowing the said still & still cap to be the property of the plaintiff and of right to belong and appurtain to him but contriving and intending to defraud & injure the said Plaintiff in this behalf yet delivered the said still and still cap to the plaintiff tho often thereto requested and has hereunto wholly refused to do. And afterwards (to wit) on the   day of   in the year aforesaid at Lebanon aforesaid converted & disposed of the said still and Still cap to his own use to the damage of the Plaintiff $150 and therefore he brings suit.

Foster for Plaintiff

(P-175)

At said June Term 1817   ) Continued by
The deft pleads not guilty & issue   ) Consent of said Term

Hadly for defendant

At September Term 1817 came the parties aforesaid by their attornies
and also a jury of good and lawful men (to wit) Wm Babb, Wm. Donnell,
Baker Wrather, Wm. Clifton, Lemuel Moor, Thomas Stone, Ebenezer Hern,
Thomas Bonner, Rich^d. Hankins, Bennett Organ, Eli Harris, & Thomas Brevard,
who being elected tried and sworn the truth to speak upon the issue joined,
retired from the bar to consult of their verdict afterwards returned into
Court and said they could not agree whereupon the parties agree to a mistrial & continued to next court.

At December Term 1817, continued

At February Term 1818, came the parties by their attornies and also a
jury of good and lawful men to wit. Wm. Babb, Uriah Cross, William Allen,
Joseph Trout, Sterling Tarpley, Joseph Cole, Thomas Hern, George Pyrtle,
Robert Bumpass, Benjamin F. Bonner, Henry Freeman, & Thomas Denton who being elected tried and sworn the truth to speak upon the issue joined upon
their oaths do say they find for the plaintiff and assess his damage to
thirty five dollars. It is therefore considered by the Court that the
Plaintiff recover of the defendant the sum of thirty five dollars his damages aforesaid by the Jurors aforesaid assessed also his cost of suit in
this behalf expended from which Judgement the defendant prayed and obtained
an appeal to the next Circuit Court to be holden for the County of Wilson
at the Court house in Lebanon on the fourth Monday in April next who entered into bond as the law directs filed reasons &c.

Bill of Costs.	
Clerks fees writ law tax and bonds	202½
Judgement 100 cts 3 subpoenas 60 cts	160
Appeal bond 60 Copy record 60 seal 80	200
Two Continuances 40 cts each	80
	6.42½
Shffs fees arrest & bond	125 cts
7 subpoenas 175 cents	
Calling cause & impaneling 2 Juries 32 cts	3.32
Attorney E. H. Foster	2.50
Ransom King a witness	2 00
Simpson Organ #	5.50
William Williams,	3.50
Soloman Williams	1.50
William Coe	5 00
Amount	$ 29.74½

(P-176) Pleas before the court of pleas and quarter sessions began and
held for the County of Wilson at the Court house in the town of Lebanon
on the first Monday in Feby. 1818 and of the Independence of the United
States the forty second.

WILLIAM HARDY   PLFT.   )
      VS.   ) Tresspass on the case
IGNATIUS JONES   DEFT.   )

    Be it remembered that heretofore (to wit) on the third Monday in June
1817 Ignatius Jones was attached to answer William Hardy in a plea of tresspass on the Case to his damage three hundred dollars.

    Whereupon the said William Hardy by William Hadly Esquire his attorney
came into court at said June term 1817 and filed his declaration in the following words and figures (to wit)

STATE OF TENNESSEE WILSON COUNTY William Hardy by his attorney Complains
of Ignatius Jones in custody &c of a plea of trespass on the case for that
whereas the said plaintiff saith that on the __ day of June 1815 in the
County aforesaid a certain conversation was moved and had between him &
the said plaintiff and him the said defendant of and concerning the lending of a quantty of corn by him the said plaintiff to the said defendant
and upon that discourse it was then & there agreed between them that the
said plaintiff should lend to the said defendant twenty barrels of corn
for one year in consideration that the plaintiff then and there at the
special instance & request of the said defendant did lend to the said defendant said twenty barrels of corn the said defendant assumed upon himself and to the plaintiff then and there faithfully promised to return to
the said plaintiff the same number of barrels of corn in one year from
the time he received the twenty barrels from the plaintiff.

    And for that whereas the said plaintiff & Defendant on the day of
April 1816 in the (P-177) County aforesaid in a certain other conversation which was moved and had between them the said plaintiff and defendant of and concerning the lending of a quanity of corn by the plaintiff to
the defendant and upon that discourse it was then and there agreed between
them that the said plaintiff should lend to the said defendant fifty seven
tubs of corn each tub holding one bushel and a half and one gallon, for
one year in consideration that the plaintiff then and there at the special
instance & request of the said defendant, did lend to the said defendant
the said fifty seven tubs of corn each tub holding one bushel and a half &
one gallon the said defendant assumed upon himselp to the plaintiff then
and there faithfully promised to return to the plaintiff the same number
of bushels of corn within one year from the time he borrowed the said
fifty seven tubs of corn.

    And for that whereas the said defendant on the __ of April 1817 in
the County aforesaid was indebted to the plaintiff in the sum of one hundred dollars for fifty seven tubs of corn each tub holding one bushel & a
half & one gallon sold to the said defendant by the said plaintiff at his
special instance & request and being so indebted the said defendant in
consideration there of afterwards (to wit) the same day and year last
aforesaid and in the County aforesaid undertook and then and there faithfully promised the said plaintiff to pay him the said sum of one hundred

dollars when he the said defendant should thereunto be requested and for that afterwards (to wit) on the day of April 1817 in the County aforesaid in consideration that the said plaintiff at the like special instance and request of him said defendant had before that time sold and delivered to the said defendant fifty seven tubs of corn each tub holding one bushel and a half & one gallon he the said defendant undertook & then & there faithfully promised (P-178) to pay the the said plaintiff so much money as the said fifty seven tubs were reasonably worth when he the said defendant should be thereunto afterwards requested and the said plaintiff avers that he therefore reasonably deserved to have of the defendant the sum of one hundred dollars whereof the said defendant afterwards (to wit) on the day and year last aforesaid had notice - nevertheless the said defendant not regarding his said several promises & undertakings made in the manner & form aforesaid but contriving & fraudulently intending craftily & subtilly to deceive and defraud the Plaintiff in this behalf hath not kept and performed His promises and undertakings aforesaid altho often requested but hath entirely refused and still doth refuse to keep & perform the same to the damage of the plaintiff three hundred dollars and therefore he sues &c.

                    Hadly atto.

at said June Term 1817

     The defendant pleads non assumpsit

                    Foster Atto =

     From said June Term this suit is continued until February Term 1817 and thereupon came the parties aforesaid by their attornies also a jury of good & lawful men (to wit) William Babb, George Pyrtle, Henry Freeman, Joseph Cole, William Allen, James Stone, George H. Bullard, Martin Talley, Thomas Turnham, William Walker, George Penny, and Edward D. Traylor, who being elected tried and sworn the truth to speak upon the issue joined upon their oaths do say the defendant did assume upon himself in manner and form as the plaintiff in declaring hath alledged and assess his damages by reason thereof to fifty seven dollars and forty cents.

     It is therefore considered by the Court that the said plaintiff recover of the said defendant the damages aforesaid by the Jury aforesaid in form aforesaid assessed amounting to fifty seven dollars & forty cents, and also his costs by him about his suit in this behalf expended and that said defendant &c.

     From which Judgement the defendant (P-179) prays an appeal to the next Circuit Court to be holden for the County of Wilson at the Court house in Lebanon on the fourth Monday in April next, entered into bond filed reasons &c and there upon an appeal is granted.

          Bill of Costs
     Clerks fee writ law tax & prosecution bond $202½

One continuance 40 cts 5 spas at 20 cts each	1.40
Judgement 100 cts copy record 60 seals 80	2.40
Sheriff Fees one arrest & bond	1 25
Executing 14 subpoenas @ 25 cts each	3 25
Calling cause & Jury	10
Attorney William Hadly	2 50
	$12.98½

Witness Costs

Ransom Gwyn a witness for Plaintiff	2.50
Stephen Yarnell do "	2.50
William Hamilton " "	3.00
Dandridge Moss, " "	2.50
Abraham Hughly, " "	3.00
Nicholers Hapson " "	2.50
Alexander Hamilton " "	2.50
Hugh Telford a witness for the Deft.	2.00
Thomas Jones witness for deft.	2.94
J. Thompson " " "	.50
Osburn Thompson	1.50
John Hannah " "	3.50
Brien McDermit, " "	2.00
Alexander Brightwell "	12.90
John C. Hannah	3.00
Stephen Barton	2.50
Total amt. of Cost	61.32½

(P-180)   Pleas before the Court of pleas and Quarter sessions began and
held for the County of Wilson at the Court house in the town of Lebanon on
the third Monday in December 1816 and 41st year of American Independence.

```
    JOHN W. PAYTON  ADMR. OF        )
JAMES SCOTT  PLFT.                  )
    VS.                             )
    DAVID IRRIS  ADMR. OF           )
JOHN IRWIN,   DEFT                  )        In covt.
```

Be it remembered that heretofore (to wit) on the third Monday in December 1816 David Irwin adm- of John Irwin was attached to answer John W.
Payton administrator of James Scott of a plea of covenant broken to his
damage five hundred dollars.

At said December Term 1816 a rule of court was entered on the Docket
thus, continued for want of decleration at March Term 1817 Continued for
want of decleration time to declare so as not to delay trial at next term.

At June Term 1817 continued under former rule. at September Term 1817
Rule plead and try on demurer & try so as not to delay trial.

At December Term 1817 came the plaintiff by his attorney Epraim H.
Foster, esquire and filed his decleration in the following words & figures

(to wit)

STATE OF TENNESSEE) December
WILSON COUNTY   ) sessions 1817

John W. Payton admr. of all & singular the goods and chattels of James
Scott decd. by Atto. complains of David Irwin Admr. of John Irwin in Custody &c in a plea of covenant broken for that whereas by certain deed of
indenture made at ___ in the County aforesaid on the 10th day of February
in the year 1804 between the said James in his life time of the one part,
and the said John in his life time of the other, sealed with the seal of
the said John and here now in Court to be produced it was witnessed among
other things for in consideration of the sum of $100 to the said John
paid in hand by the said James the said John had granted bargained sold and
conveyed to the said James and his heirs &c forever a certain tract or parcel of land lysing & being in the County aforesaid containing four hundred
and two acres on Spring Creek (P-181) Begining at a hackberry and sugar
tree, thence west 86 poles to Donnells line thence south 93 poles & 1/2 to
a beech thence west 234 poles to a stake thence south 227 poles to a stake
thence East 193 poles to a sugar tree it being James Bones south west corner thence north 127 poles to a white hickory thence East 127 poles to a
beech thence north 193 poles to the beginning being a part of a 640 acre
tract part of which said tract said Irwin sold to James Barrers, and James
Stewart which tract of 640 was granted to Thomas Hickman & by him sold to
said Irwin to have and to hold the same to the said James with the appurtenances his heirs & assigns forever and the said John by the deed aforesaid further covenanted with the said James with other things the above
tract of land & bargained promises he would warrant & forever defend against
the claim of all persons whatsoever and the said plaintiff in fact says that
the said John in his life time did not keep his said covenant with the said
James in his life time but hath broken the same in this that heretofore (to
wit) in the life time of the said James on the 27th day of February in the
year 1812 an action of ejectment was commenced in the Court of pleas &
quarter sessions for the County aforesaid by John Den, lessee of George
Donnell against Samuel Scott tenant in possesion under claim of the said
James in his life time for the land aforesaid wherein the said John claimed
by virtue of a better adverse title to which said action the said James being admitted Co- Deft by a rule of said court at March Term 1812 pleaded not
guilty and thereupon an issue was joined & the Cause was so continued & proceeded in that on the day of June in the year 1815 by the verdict of a jury
& the Judgement & consideration of said Court the said James was cast in
the Action aforesaid & the said John lessee as aforesaid recovered 65 acres
of said land whereby the said James was evicted ejected & removed from 68
acres of said land and whereby the said John failed to defend the title as
aforesaid of all of which the said John then & there had notice in his lifetime and also that at the execution of the deed aforesaid (P-182) the
said John had no good and sufficient title to the said 65 acres part of said
402 acres but one George Donnell was then and there the owner there of by
virtue of a better adverse legal claim in the said Donnell by virtue of which
he had since by due course of law evicted & ejected the said James in his
life there from and also in this that the said John in his life time nor the

said David Administrator as aforesaid since the death of the said John have
not warranted & defended the right and title of the said James in his life
time to said - acres of land part of said 40 acres nor to the Plaintiff since
his death against the claims of all persons whatsoever, and so the said
Plaintiff says that the covenants aforesaid are broken in manner & form aforesaid and to keep & perform the same to the said James in his life, the said
John in in his life time and the said David since the said John's death
wholly refused and failed and since the death of the said James the said
John in his lifetime and the said David since his death have wholly refused
the covenant aforesaid with the said plaintiff and the said David still
wholly rejects and refuses to keep the covenant aforesaid with the Plaintiff
since the death of the said James to his damage $500 and therefore he brings
his suit

Foster atto. for Plaintiff.

And the Defendant at said December Term last mentioned came into Court
and defends the wrong & injury then &c. & for plea in this behalf said
David saith that he ought not to have and maintain his said action thereof
against him because he saith that the said John in his life time and the
said David since his death hath well and truly performed all his covenants
with the said James in said declaration mentioned and this he is ready to
verify & therefore he prays judgement

J. J. White for Plaintiff.

issue joined Foster

And for further plea the said David saith that the said John W. ought not to
have and (P-183) maintain his said action because protesting that at
the time of unsealing & delivering of said deed the said tract or parcel of
land was free from any incumberance what soever he saith that said land was
not covered by the lawful claim & title of George Donnell of higher legal
dignity than the title of him the said John in manner & form as said John
W. in assigning said breach of covenant hath alledged & of this he puts
himself upon the County.

Issue Foster

J. J. White Atto Plaintiff.

At February Term 1818 came the parties aforesaid by their attornies
also a jury of good & lawful men (to wit) William Hartsfield, James Stone,
Simpson Organ, Notly Maddox, Benjamin T. Motly, Jonathan Doak, Soloman
Williams, Thomas Turnham, John W. Nichols, Laden Shepherd, & John Garrison,
John Turnham, who being elected tried and sworn the truth to speak upon
the issue joined upon their oaths do say they find the defendant hath not
kept and performed his covenant as the plaintiff in his declaration hath
alledged and assess the damage of the plaintiff occasioned by the breach
of the covenant to two hundred and thirty nine dollars & twenty five cents.

It is therefore considered by the Court that said plaintiff recover
against the said defendant the sum of two hundred and thirty nine dollars

and twenty five Cents the damages aforesaid by the Jurors aforesaid assessed Also his cost of suit in this behalf expended.

And the defendant in mercy &c

      Bill of Cost

Clerks fees writ law tax & bond	2.02½
3 Continuances at 40 cts each	1.20
Judgement & record	1.00
Sheriff arrest calling Cause & jury	1.16
	5 38½
Atto. B. H. Foster	6 25
	$11.63½

(P-184)   Pleas before the Court of pleas and quarter sessions began and held for the County of Wilson at the Court house in the Town of Lebanon on Monday the 17th day of June 1816 & 40th Year of Am. Independence.

ROBERT DONELSON   PLFT.)
      VS   ) In Case
EDMUND GREENAGE   DEFT.)

Be it remembered that heretofore to wit, at March term 1816 Edmund Greenage was attached to answer Robert Donelson, of a plea of trespass on the case and at June Term 1816 Judgement was rendered for the plaintiff and an appeal taken to the Circuit Court see the records of June Term 1816 in this book recorded.

      Bill of Costs of witnesses &c

William Thomas a witness proved 5 days & 34 miles	$6,36
Richard Ramsey 5 days	2.50
William Bradberry 4 days	2.00
Robert Fullerton 5 days	2.50
Recd. my fee Robert Fullerton.	
James Bradberry 5 days	2.50
William Sands 3 days	1.50
Joshua Kelly 5 days	2.50
Humphrey Donelson 3 days	1.50

(P-185) Pleas before the Court of Pleas and quarter sessions at the Court house in Lebanon on the first Monday May 1818 & 42nd year of our Independence.

FRANCIS & DAVID BELL   PLFT.)
      VS.   ) In debt
GEORGE CUMMINS   DEFT.   )

Be it remembered that heretofore a writ issue returnable to said May term in the following words and figures (to wit)

STATE OF TENNESSEE   to the sheriff of Wilson County greetings—
    You are hereby commanded to take the body of George Cummings, if to be found in your County and him safely keep so that you have him before the Justice

of our ensuing Court of pleas and quarter sessions to be held for the County of Wilson at the Court house in town of Lebanon on the first Monday in May next, then & there to answer Francis Bell and David Bell in a plea that they he render unto them one thousand dollars which to them he owes and from them unjustly detains to their damage one hundred dollars herein fail not and have you then there this writ

Witness John Allcorn Clerk of our said Court at office this first Monday in February 1818 and in the 42nd year of Am. Independence

John Allcorn Clerk.

I acknowledge myself the plaintiffs security in the sum of two hundred dollars for prosecuting the above writ with effect or payment of all cost and damages incident failure thereof witness my hand and seal this 27th day of April 1818.

Ephriam H. Foster.

Issued 27th April 1818

Came the hand the same day issued Executed.

Thos Bradley Shff.

(P-186)   At May Term 1818 an entry stands on the appearance Docket (thus) time to Declare

At August Term 1818 an entry is made on the docket thus-
This cause is by consent transfered to the Circuit Court but will not stand for trial at that term unless a decleration is handed to Defendants Counsel at February County Court.

of the County to wit At February Term 1819 the Plaintiff by his attorney comes into Court and files his decleration in the following words and figures (to wit)

STATE OF TENNESSEE)   Court of Pleas & quarter sessions
WILSON COUNTY   )   February Term 1819

Francis Bell & David Bell by their attornies complain of George Cummings in custody &c in a plea that he render to them the sum of one thousand dollars which to them he owes and from them unjustly detains - For that the said George Cummings on the 17th day of November 1815 (to wit) at Lebanon in the County aforesaid by his certain writing obligatory of that date sealed with his seal and here in Court ready to be produced bound and acknowledged himself to be indebted to the said Francis David Bell & David Bell in the said sum of one thousand dollars to be paid to them when thereto requested yet though often requested the said George Cummings hath never paid the same or any part thereof to the said plaintiff but to do the same hath hitherto wholly refused and still refuses to the damage of the said Frances Bell and David Bell one thousand Dollars and therefore they sue & thereon pledges &c.

Foster for Plaintiff

Bill of Costs, writ law tax &c	3.02½
Transcript and Seal	1.40
Shff. Bradley	1 25
Sucefful atto.	2.50
isd. 5th March Clerks	
Certificate follows 1819	$ 8.17½

(P187) Pleas before the Court of pleas and quarter sessions held for the
County of Wilson in the State of Tennessee at the Court house in Lebanon on
the first Monday in November in the year 1818.

GIDEON HUGHES   PLFT.)
        VS.   ) In Case
BURCHET DOUGLAS   DEFT.)

        Be it remembered that heretofore to wit as May Term 1818 of said Court
Burchett Douglass was attached to answer Gideon Hughs of a plea of tresspass on the case whereupon the said Gideon Hughs by his attorney ~~complains~~
Ephriam H. Foster esquire filed his decleration in the words and figures
following (to wit)

STATE OF TENNESSEE
WILSON COUNTY   May Term 1818

        Gideon Hughs by his attorney Complains of Burchett Douglass in custody
&c of a plea of tresspass on the Case, for that the said Burchett Douglass
defendant at ____ on the ____ day of ____ in the County aforesaid in consideration that the said Gideon Hughs at the special request of the said Burchett
before that time done and performed certain work and labor in building a boat
& furnishing material therefor for the benefit of the said Burchett promised
to pay the plaintiff on demand so much money as he reasonably deserves to
have therefor and the plaintiff avers that he reasonably deserves to have
therefor the sum of two hundred dollars, of which the said Burchett then and
there had notice, and for that whereas at - in the county aforesaid on the
same day and year aforesaid the said defendant being indebted to the plaintiff in one other sum of two hundred dollars for certain work & labor done
and performed by the plaintiff before that time in building a boat for the
said defendant at his request and for divers timbers and materials found &
provided by the plaintiff in and about such boat at the like request of
said Defendant in Consideration whereof the defendant promised to pay on
demand the said sum when requested (P-188) and for that whereas in the
county aforesaid on the same day and year aforesaid the said plaintiff has
performed certain work and labor in building a boat and furnishing materials
at the special instance and request of the said defendant, who then and
there promised to pay the plaintiff therefor on demand so much money as the
same was reasonably worth and the plaintiff avers that the same at the time
and place aforesaid reasonably worth one other sum of two hundred dollars
of which the said defendant had then and there notice And for that whereas
at ____ in the county aforesaid on the same day & year aforesaid the defendant being indebted to the plaintiff in one other sum of two hundred dollars
for so much money before that time had and received by said defendant to

the Plaintiffs use in consideration thereof then and there promised the plaintiff to pay him the said sum on demand and for that whereas afterwards to wit at __ in the County aforesaid on the same day and year aforesaid the defendant being indebted to the plaintiff in one other sum of two hundred dollars for so much money before that time but and accommodated by the plaintiff of the said defendant at his request in consideration thereof promised ~~to pay~~ the plaintiff to pay him the same on demand and for that whereas the said defendant & plaintiff at __ in the county aforesaid on the same day and year aforesaid accounted to-gether and of & concerning their mutual dealings and of and concerning divers sums of money due before that time from said defendant to said plaintiff and thereupon said Defendant was found indebted & in arrears to the said plaintiff in one other sum of two hundred dollars in consideration thereof the said defendant then and there promised the plaintiff to pay him the same sum on demand yet tho often requested the said defendant has never paid the same but wholly neglects and refuses so to do to the damage of the plaintiff two hundred dollars

Foster   Atto.

(P-189)   and thereupon the defendant comes and pleads non assumpset & Statue of limitations

Hadly atto. for deft.   and issue is joined
And the said course was continued from time untill this term (to wit) the time just above mentioned and now at this time came the parties by their Attornies & also a jury of good and lawful min (to wit) Hardy Hunt, James Thompson, William Donnell, Seth P. Pool, John B. Turnham, John Stone, Jonathan Ozment, John Smart, James Stone, William Johnson, Robert W. Pool, & Robert Donelson, who being elected tried and sworn the truth to speak upon the issue joined upon their oaths do say the said Defendant did assume upon himself in manner and form as plaintiff in declaring hath alledged and assess his damages to ninety dollars.

It is therefore considered by the court that said Plaintiff recover of the Defendant the Damages aforesaid by the jurors aforesaid in form aforesaid assessed and also his cost by him about his suit in this behalf expended From which Judgement the defendant prays an appeal to the Circuit Court and on filing reasons and entering into bond with security conditioned as the law directs the same is granted.

```
          Bill of Cost
          Writ law tax & bond    140            302 cts
          1 continuance 40,  2 subpoenas  40 pro-
          bate 10 witnesses 60  Judgement 100
          Transcript & seal 40                  $682½
          Sheriff arrest & bond 125   executing
            subpoena  25                         150
          Atto  Foster                           250
          Isaac Doaks  a witness  4 days  26 miles    504
```

Edward Douglass	6 do	48	do		792
George Martin	4 do				200
George Cooper	6 do	80	do		920
Daniel Propps	8 do	72	do		1088
John Cornegy	4 do	26	do		504
Barney Cornegy	4 do	26	do		504

I John Allcorn Clk. &c do cerlify &c.

(P-190) Pleas before the court of pleas and quarter sessions began and held for the County of Wilson at the Court house in Lebanon on the first Monday in February 1819 & 43rd year of Am. Independence.

TAOMAS TI TIMMONN ANNIONNN)
                    VS.   ) IA AMMI
IIIIIAM AAIIMM DEFT)

JAMES WYNNE   PLFT.)
           VS   ) In case
JOEL ECHOLS)

Be it remembered that here to fore to wit at August Term 1818 of said Court Joel Echols was attached to answer James T. Wynne of a plea of tresspass on the case to his damage three hundred dollars whereupon the said plaintiff by his attorney filed his declaration in the words & figures following (to wit)   State of Tennessee Wilson County August sessions 1818 James T. Wynne by his attorney complains of Joel Echols, in custody &c of a plea of tresspass on the case for that whereas on the ____ day of January 1818 the said Joel Echols in the County aforesaid was indebted to the said James T. Wynne, in the sum of one hundred and seven dollars and fifty cents lawful money of this State for so much money by the said James T. Wynne before that time paid laid out & expended to and for the use of the said Joel Echols & his special instance and request and being so indebted he the said Joel Echols in consideration thereof afterwards to wit, on the day and year last aforesaid in the County of Wilson aforesaid undertook and then and there faithfully promised to pay said James T. Wynne the last mentioned sum of money when he the said Joel should be thereunto afterwards requested and whereas also the said Joel Echols afterwards (to wit) on the day and year last aforesaid in the County of Wilson aforesaid was indebted to the said James T. Wynne, in the further sum of one hundred & seven dollars and fifty cents of like lawful money of this State for so much (P-191) money before that time lent and advanced to the said defendant at his special instance and request and being so indebted he the said defendant in consideration thereof afterwards (to wit) on the day and year last aforesaid in the County aforesaid undertook & then and there faithfully promised the said plaintiff to pay him the said last mentioned sum of money when he the said defendant should be thereunto afterwards requested nevertheless the said defendant not regarding his said promises & undertakings made in manner and form aforesaid hath not paid the plaintiff the said sum of one hundred AIII and seven dollars and fifty Cents spoken of in the 1st & 2nd Court or any part thereof but the same to pay hath wholy refused & still refuses to pay the same to the damage of the plaintiff three hundred dollars and therefore he brings suit Hadley atto P. 2. and the defendant by his attorney comes and defends the wrong and injury when and where &c every thing else he ought to defend and for plea says he did not assume upon himself in manner and form as the plaintiff in declaring hath alledged and of this he puts himself upon the County & pleads payment S. Anderson atto. and the Plaintiff likewise,

Hadly atto P.2

And the said cause was continued from term to term until the term first above mentioned and now at this day came the parties by their attornies & thereupon came a jury of good and lawful men (to wit) Lewis Chambers, Benjamin Winford, Joseph Weir, Coleman Stone, Daniel Moser John Allen Allen, William Wilson, Edward Truvilion, William Hollingsworth, Joseph Mullenax John Bond & Robert Bumpass, who being elected tried and sworn the truth to speak upon the issue joined upon their oaths do say the defendant did assume upon himself in manner and form as the plaintiff in declaring hath alledged, and assess his damages by reason thereof to one hundred and thirteen dollars eighty seven and a half cents, and the plaintiff remits seven dollars eighty seven and a half cents of the said damages assessed whereupon it is considered by the Court that the said plaintiff recover of the Defendant the balance of the damages aforesaid by the jurors aforesaid in form aforesaid assessed amounting to one hundred and six dollars and also his costs about his suit in this behalf expended (P-192) expended From which judgement the defendant prays an appeal to the Circuit Court, and on filing reasons and entering into bond with security conditioned as the law directs the same is granted.

```
     Bill of Costs
writ    /// /// & bond 140  tax 162½  1 Continuance 40
    cents  1 spa. 20  Judgement 100 transcript & seal  140    602½
Sheriff arrest and bond                                       125
Sheriff Douglass executing spa.                               25
atto. Hadly                                                   250
Charles Watkins  a witness                                   309
                                                          $13.11½
```

SAMUEL W. SHERRELL PLFT.)
        VS.   ) In Case
BRITTAIN DRAKE DEFT.   )

Be it remembered that heretofore (to wit) at August Term 1818 of said Court Brittain Drake, was attached to answer Samuel W. Sherrell, of a plea of tresspass on the Case and there upon the said Samuel W. Sherrell, by H. L. Douglass, his attorney filed his decleration in the words & figures following (to wit)

STATE OF TENNESSEE WILSON COUNTY COURT August Term 1818 Samuel W. Sherrell by his attorney complains of Brittain Drake, in Custody &c of a plea of tresspass on the case for that whereas the said Brittain Drake, on the __ day of __ in the year 1818 at Lebanon in the County aforesaid

upon a certain conversation then and there had with the said plaintiff of
and concerning a certain negro woman slave the property of one Thomas
Harrington, which the said plaintiff ~~which the said plaintiff~~ held by
mortgage as security for the payment of __ dollars before that loaned &
advanced to the said Thomas by said plaintiff he the said Brittain in consideration that the said plaintiff at the special instance & request of the
said Brittain would release and give up to the said Harrington the said
slave, then and there undertook and promised said plaintiff that two ~~notes~~
certain notes commonly called post notes for one hundred dollars each
purpoting to be payable by the president & directors of the Kentucky Insurance Company signed by Wm. H. Richardson, Prest. and J. L. Martin,
Cash which he the said Brittain then and there paid to the said plaintiff
in consideration aforesaid (P-193) aforesaid were good and current
money and worth two hundred dollars and that the said plaintiff could not
pay them, or if they were not good he the said Brittain would pay to
said plaintiff said sum of two hundred dollars, and said plaintiff avers
that he did then and there release and give up to the said Harrington
said slave of which said Brittain then and there had notice and said
plaintiff further in fact says that said notes were not good & current
money but that they were with nothing of which said Brittain afterwards
to wit on the __ day of ___ 1818 at the County aforesaid had notice yet
said Brittain not regarding his aforesaid promise & undertaking but contriving and intending to injure & defraud the said Plaintiff hath not
paid the aforesaid sum of two hundred dollars nor any part thereof tho
repeatedly required so to do but the same to pay hath and still doth refuse to his damage three hundred dollars.

                                        Douglass atto.

and there upon the said defendant by his attorney pleads non assumpset &
puts himself upon the Country.

                        S. Anderson
                and the Plaintiff likewise

Douglass for plft.

And the cause was continued from term to term untill this term to wit
the term first above mentioned and now at this day it being the second
day of the term came the parties by their attornies & also a jury of
good and lawful men to wit   Lewis Chambers, Benjamin Winford, Joseph
Weir, Colman Stone, Donnel Moser, John Allen, William Wilson, Edward
Truvillion, William Hollingsworth, Joseph Mullinax, John Bond & Robert
Bumpass who being elected tried and sworn the truth to speak upon the
issue joined upon their oaths do say the defendant did assume upon himself in manner and form as the plaintiff in declaring hath alledged &
assess his damage by reason thereof to two hundred dollars

    It is therefore considered by the Court that the said plaintiff re-
cover against the Defendant the damages aforesaid by the jury in form
aforesaid assessed and also his costs about his suit in this behalf ex-

pended. From which (P-194) which judgement the defendant prays an appeal and on ƒ/ƒ/ƒ/ƒ filing reasons and entering into bond with security conditioned as the law directs it is granted.

```
     Bill of Cost
     Clerks fee  merit and bond             140
     law tax 162½ one continuance 40 judge-
     ment 100, Transcript and seal  140     582½
     Sheriff arrest & Bond                  125
     Atto  Douglass,                        250
     Benton Modglin  a witness              200
     Transcript issued 8th                $11.57½
     February 1819.
```

ABRAM MCGEHEE   PLFT.)
        VS   ) Appeal
WILLIAM N. SLATE DEFT.)

Be it remembered that on the first day of the term above mentioned the papers in the above suit were filed with the Clerk in open Court & are in the words and figures following (to wit)

STATE OF TENNESSEE)
WILSON COUNTY   ) To any lawful officer to execute and return summon William N. Slate to appear before some justice for said County to answer the Complaint of Abram McGehe in a plea of Debt due by account, here in fail not and a due return make given under my hand & seal the 25th day of November 1818.

                          Joseph L. Bell (J.P.)

And on the back of said warrant were the following endorsements executed by T. Harris Const- Plaintiff and Defendant appearing and the witnesses being sworn & examined an judgement is that the plaintiff take nothing by this warrant and pay the cost of said suit 27th Oct. 1818

                          A. C. Carruth   J.P.
                          John Bonner   J.P.
                          Jos. T. Bell   J.P.

An appeal prayed and granted to the plaintiff who inters into bond with Seth P. Pool his security. and now at this day being (P-195) being the fourth day of the term first above mentioned came the parties by their attornies and also a jury of good and lawful men (to wit) Coleman Stone, Lewis Chambers, William Wilson, Daniel Moser, Edward Truvillion Joseph Weir, John Allen, William Draper, Patrick Higety, Joseph Cole, Elisha Brien, & Benjamin Winford, who being elected tried and sworn to try the appeal between the parties aforesaid upon their oaths do say they find for the plaintiff thirty five dollars besides his cost. It is therefore considered by the Court that the said plaintiff recover of the said defendant the said sum of thirty five dollars so found by the jurors aforesaid, And also his Costs by him about his suit expended whereupon the said defendant prays an appeal to the Circuit Court files reasons for the same and entered into bond with John Bonner & Cornelius N. Lewis his securities & there upon the same is granted

Bill of Costs

Constable executing warrant	50
subp. 25 cts	$ .75
Clerks fee tax 112½ judgement 100 cts	
Transcript & seal 140 Cents	3 52½
Atto Douglass & White	1 25
James McGehe a witness	2 00
Fanny L. Liggon do	1 50
	$ 9.02½

Transcript issd. 17th February 1819

(P-196)

```
JOHN DEN    LESSEE     )
       VS.             )  In Ejectment
SAMUEL CLEMMONS  DEFT. )
```

Be it remembered that heretofore (to wit) at February Term 1818 of said court Samuel Clemmons, was attached to answer John Dew Lessee of John Donelson of a plea wherefore with forse and arms he broke and entered the close of the said Plaintiff and ejected him there from whereupon the said plaintiff by his attorney filed his decleration in the words and figures following (to wit)

STATE OF TENNESSEE   WILSON COUNTY

John Doe by his attorney complains of Richard Roe in Custody &c of a plea of tresspass & Ejectment for that whereas John Donelson in the present year eighteen hundred & eighteen at the County of Wilson aforesaid had demised to the said John Doe a certain tenement tract or parcel of land with the appurtenances by containing six hundred and forty acres on the first Creek east of Pond lick Creek Beginning where the said Donnelson's upper line of a survey No.2710 crosses the same thence along his line south one hundred and sixty poles to a red oak.

thence East three hundred and twenty poles to two dogwoods thence north three hundred & twenty poles Crossing the said creek to a stake thence west three hundred and twenty poles to a stake thence south to the beginning No. of grant 2714 dated 20th July 1796 to have and to hold to the said John Doe, and his heirs & assigns from the tenth day of January in the present year eighteen hundred & eighteen untill the full end & term of five years next ensuing and fully to be compleated & ended.

By virtue of which demise the said John Doe entered into the said tenements with the appurtenances and was possessed thereof and the said John being so possessed the said Richard Roe afterwards (to wit) on the said tenth day of January in the year aforesaid with force and arms entered into said tenement tract or parcel of land so demised as aforesaid for the term aforesaid, which is not yet expended and ejected him the said John Doe from his said tenement tract or parcel of (P-197) of land and other wrongs to the said John then and there did, to the great damage of the said John and against the peace and dignity of the State whereupon the said John Doe, saith he is injured & indamaged to the value of five hundred dollars & there upon he sues.

Foster atto.

Mr Samuel Clemmons, I am informed that you are in possession of or claim title to the premises in this decleration mentioned or to some part thereof and I being sued in this action as casual ejector and having no claim or title to same, do advise you to appear on the first Monday in February next at a Court to be held for the County of Wilson in the town of Lebanon by some attorney of that court and then and there by a rule of said Court to cause your self to be made defendant in my stead otherwise I shall suffer judgement to be entered against me and you will be turned out of possession. I am your loving friend Richard Roe.

And at February term aforesaid the said Samuel Clemons, is admitted defendant in the room of the Casual ejector agrees to confess lease entry ouster & on the trial to rely on the title only and pleads not guilty, and thereupon issue is joined.

May term 1818. It is ordered by the Court the parties being present & consenting there to that William Moss, be appointed to survey the lands in dispute and this cause is continued

August term 1818 by consent of the parties a Commissioer is awarded to take the Deposition of Nicholas Quesenberry on the part of the plaintiff on a notice of ten days and this cause is continued.

November term 1818 At this day came the parties by their attornies and there upon came a jury of good and lawful men (to wit) Benjamin Chapman, Charles White, Thomas Parham, George Avery, Henry Reeff, Beverly Williams, William Walker, John Curry, Alexander Richmond, Milberry Hern Martin Tally, & Notley Madox who being elected tried and sworn the truth to speak upon the issue joined upon their oathes do say the defendant is not guilty of the tresspass & ejectment in manner and form as the plaintiff in declaring hath alledged.

It   (P-198)   It is therefore considered by the Court that the said defendant go hence without day and recover against the plaintiff, this costs about his defence in this behalf expended.

From which judgement the plaintiff prays an appeal to the next Circuit Court to be held for the County of Wilson at the Court house in Lebanon on the fourth Monday in April next and on entering into bond with security and filing reasons for the same.

It is by the Court here granted.

Bill of Costs
Clerks writ & Bond 149 tax 162½ rule admitting defendant 24 order for commission
25
Commission 20, continuance 40 judgement

100 transcript & seal 140 cents	$ 6.50
Sheriff arrest & bond service of Dec.	2.00
Atto Hadley,	$ 6.25
	$14.75

(P-199)   Pleas before the Court of pleas and quarter sessions began and held for the County of Wilson at the Court house in the town of Lebanon on the first Monday in May 1819 and 43rd Year of American Independence

JOHN BONNER   PLFT.)
    VS.   ) Tresspass on
JOSEPH IRBY   DEFT.) the case

Be it remembered that there to fore (to wit) on the 26th day of October 1818 Joseph Irby was attached to answer John Bonner, of a plea of tresspass on the case to his damage two hundred dollars whereupon the said John Bonner, at November term 1818 by Harry L. Douglass, esquire his attorney came into Court and filed his decleration in the following words and figures to wit.

State of Tennessee Wilson County Court November term 1818 John Bonner, by his attorney complains of Joseph Irby in custody &c of a plea of tresspass on the case for that the said Joseph on the __ day of ____ 1818 at the County aforesaid upon a certain conversation then and there had with the said Plaintiff of and concerning a flat bottomed boat which the said plaintiff then owned and had before that time agreed to sell to a certain James Henderson, for the sum of ____ dollars he the said Joseph in consideration that the said plaintiff would sell to the said Joseph & James Jointly the said flat bottomed boat then and there undertook and promised said plaintiff that a certain bank note for one Hundred dollars purpoting to be payable by the president and directors of the Kentucky insurance Company signed by W. H. Richardson, prest. J. L. Martin Cash which the said Joseph then and there paid to said plaintiff as part price of said boat were good & current money and worth one hundred dollars and if said plaintiff could not pass it or if it was not good he the said Joseph (P-200) Joseph would pay said plaintiff one hundred dollars and said plaintiff avers that he did then and there at the special instance and request of the said Joseph sell and deliver to said Joseph & James said flat bottomed boat and said plaintiff further in fact says that said note was not good & current money but that it was worth nothing of which the said Joseph afterwards (to wit) on the __ day of ____ 1818 at the County afterwards had notice yet the said Joseph not regarding his aforesaid promise & undertaking but contriving and intending to injure & defraud the said plaintiff hath not paid said sum of one hundred dollars nor any part thereof, tho often requested but to pay the same hath and still doth refuse to his damage _____ dollars & therefore he sues &c

Douglass Atto.

And the defendant pleads non assumpset & statue of limitations & puts himself upon the County & the plff. doth the same—

S. Anderson Atto.

And the cause was continued from term untill this term (to wit) May term 1819 and not at this term came the parties by their attornies & also a jury of good and lawful men to wit, Reuben Rider, Samuel Motheral, Jacob Vantrease, William Stafford, David Billings, James Ross, Henry Carson, Simpson Organ, Jacob H. Thomas, Petter Raglin, Silas Chapman, and Joseph Cole who being elected tried & sworn the truth to speak upon the issue joined upon their oaths do say they find the said defendant did assume upon himself within three years before the bringing of this suit as the plaintiff in his decleration hath alledged and assess the damage of the plaintiff to one hundred & seven dollars and twenty five cents. It is there fore considered by the Court that the (P-201) the said plaintiff recover against the defendant the sum of one hundred & seven dollars and twenty five cents, the damage aforesaid by the jurors aforesaid assessed and also his cost of suit in this behalf expended.

From which judgement the defendant prays an appeal to the next Circuit Court to be held in the town of Lebanon on the 4th Monday in October next who entered into bond filed reasons &c and thereupon an appeal is granted by the Court &c

Bill of Cost.

Clerk writ law tax & prosecution bond		$ 302½
1 Continuance 40 cts 2 subponas 40 cts	80	
Judgement 100 cts appeal bond 60	160	
Transcript & Record 140 cts	140	
Sheriff arrest & bond 125 executing 2 subps. 50	175	
Calling cause & jury	16	
Atto Douglass 250 cts.	250	
Charles Lock a witness proved 5 days	250	
Thomas Bonner do -- 3 days	150	
	15.23½	

Pleas &c at May Term 1819

JOHN CARTWRIGHT   PLFT.) Tresspass
    VS.   ) on the Cost
WILLIAM HALLUM   DEFT.)

Be it remembered that heretofore to wit, on the 5th day of December 1818 William Hallum, was attached to answer John Cartwright, of a plea of tresspass on the Case to his damage two hundred and fifty dollars whereupon the said John Cartwright, by Harry L. Douglass, esquire his attorney came into Court at February Term 1819 and filed his decleration in the following words and figures (to wit)

(turn over)

(P-202)   State of Tennessee Wilson County Court of pleas & quarter sessions February Term 1819 -

John Cartwright by his attorney Complains of William Hallum, in Custody &c of a plea of tresspass on the case For that whereas the said William on the __ day of ___ in the year of our Lord 1818 to wit at Lebanon in the County aforesaid was indebted to the said John in the sum of one hundred and eighty seven dollars and fifty cents for divers goods wares and merchandise by the said John before that time sold & delivered ~~to the said John before that time sold and delivered~~ to the said William at the special instances and request of the said William and being so indebted he the said William in consideration thereof afterwards to wit the same day & year aforesaid at Lebanon aforesaid in the County aforesaid undertook and then and there faithfully promised said John to pay him the said sum of money when he should be thereto afterwards requested and whereas afterwards towit, on the same day and year aforesaid at Lebanon aforesaid in the County aforesaid in consideration that the said John at the like request of the said William divers other goods wares & merchandise he the said William undertook and then & there faithfully promised the said John to pay him so much money as he there fore reasonably derived to have when the said William should be thereto afterwards requested and the said John avers that he therefore reasonably deserves to have of the said William other sum of one hundred & eighty seven dollars and fifty cents to wit at Lebanon aforesaid in the County aforesaid whereof he the said William afterwards to wit on the same day and year aforesaid then & there has notice and whereas afterwards (to wit) on the same day & year aforesaid, at Lebanon aforesaid in the County aforesaid the said William accounted together with the said John of & Concerning divers other sums of money from the said William to the said John before that time due and owing then and then in arears & unpaid & upon that account the said William was then and there found in arears and indebted (P-203)   to the said John in other sum of one hundred & eighty seven dollars & fifty cents, and being found in arears & indebted he the said William in consideration thereof afterwards to wit on the same day and year aforesaid at Lebanon aforesaid in the County aforesaid undertook & faithfully promised the said John to pay him the said last mentioned sum of money, when he should be thereto afterwards requested, yet the said William altho often requested hath not yet paid the said several sums of money or any part there of to the said John but to pay the same or any part thereof to the said John he the said William hath hitherto wholy refused & still refuses to pay the said John to his damage two hundred & fifty dollars therefore brings his suit & he has found pledges &c.

Douglass for the Plaintiff

Pleas non assumpset & issue William Williams for defendant

At May Term 1819, This day came the parties by their attornies and thereupon a jury of good and lawful men to wit Patrick Higarty, George White, Charles Lock, John Ray, Jacob H. Thomas, Reuben Rider, Samuel Motheral, Jacob Vantrece, James Ross, Henry Carson, Simpson Organ, & Joseph Cole who being elected tried and sworn the truth to speak upon the issue joined upon their oaths do say they find the defendant did assume upon himself in manner and form as the plaintiff in declaring against him hath alledged and assess the plaintiffs damage to one hundred & eighty seven dollars & fifty cents It is therefore considered by the Court that the said plaintiff recover against the said Defendant the damages aforesaid by the jurors aforesaid in form aforesaid assessed and also his cost of suit in this behalf expended.

From which judgement the Defendant prays an appeal to the next Circuit Court to be holden for the County aforesaid at Lebanon on the 4th Monday in October next. and upon his filing reasons for the appeal & entering into bond as the law directs an appeal is here granted.

Bill of Costs writ law tax & bond $302\frac{1}{2}$
1 spa 20 Judgement 100 transcript & seal
140 cents $5.62\frac{1}{2}$
Sheriff arrest & bond   1.25
Atto Douglass   2.50
                                                 $9.37\frac{1}{2}$

(P-204) Pleas before the Court of pleas & quarter sessions began and held for the County of Wilson at the Court house in the town of Lebanon on the first Monday in May 1819 & the 43rd year of American Independence.

THOMAS H. FLETCHER ASSIGNEE PLFT.)
      VS.   ) In Debt
WILLIAM HALLUM   DEFT.   )

Be it remembered that hereto fore (to wit) on the second day of November 1818 William Hallum was attached to answer Thomas H. Fletcher assignee of a plea that he render to him twelve hundred & fifty one dollars & seventy four cents which to him he owes & from him unjustly detains to his damage two hundred & fifty dollars.

At February Term 1819 a rule is entered on the docket plea & try ___ at May Term 1819 Came the plaintiff H. L. Douglass esquire and filed his declaration in the following words and figures (to wit)

STATE OF TENNESSEE)
WILSON COUNTY   ) Court of pleas & quarter sessions May Term 1819

Thomas H. Fletcher assignee by attorney complains of William Hallum in custody &c of a plea that he render to him twelve hundred & fifty one dollars and seventy four cents which to him he owes and from him unjustly detains For that whereas the said William Hallum by the name and discription of William Hallum made his certain bill single sealed with his seal dated the 26th day of February 1817 and thereby promised to pay John Hallum twelve hundred and fifty one dollars & seventy four cents for value received on or before the tenth day of August next, after the date there of and the said bill single of that day and date here ready to be produced to the Court & the said John Hallum to whom the payment of the said sum of money mentioned in the said note was to be made, afterwards & before the payment of the said sum contained /////// in said note or any part thereof, and also before the time appointed by the said note for the payment thereof (P-205) to wit on the __ day of ___ 1817 at the County aforesaid endorsed the said note his own proper hand /////// being thereon subscribed & by that endorsement the said John Hallum appointed the Contents of the said note to be paid to the firm of John P. Erwen & Co. and then and there delivered the said note to the said firm of John P. Erwen & Co. to whom the payment of the said sum of money mentioned in the said note was to be paid, afterwards & before the payment of the said sum of money contained in the said note or of any part thereof (to wit) on the ___ day of ___ A.D. 1817 endorsed note their own proper hand /////// being thereon subscribed & by that endorsement appointed the contents of the said note to be paid to the firm of Erwin M. Laughlin & Co and then and there delivered the said note so endorsed to the said firm Erwin McLaughlin & Co. & the said firm Erwin McLaughlin, & Co to whom the payment of the said sum of money /////// /// mentioned in said note was to be made afterwards & before the payment of the said sum of money contained in said note or any part there of, and also before the time appointed by the said note for the payment thereof (to wit) on the day of ___ A.D. 1817 at the County of Wilson aforesaid, endorsed the said note their own proper hand being thereon subscribed and by that endorsement the said firm of Erwin McLaughlin & Co appointed the Contents of the said note to be paid to the said Thomas H. Fletcher & then and there delivered the said note so endorsed to the said Thomas H. Fletcher of which said several endorsements the said William Hallum then and there had notice, viz on the day of __ A.D.1817 at the County aforesaid - By reason thereof & by force of an act of the general assembly in such Case made & provided a right a right hath accured to the said Thomas H. Fletcher to ask and have the said sum of money in said bill single mentioned never the less the said William Hallum refuses to pay the said sum to the said Thomas H. Fletcher, /// /// /// //// nor has the said Thomas H. Fletcher recovered any part thereof from the said William Hallum nor have the previous endorsers received payment of the said note or any part thereof to the said (P-206)   said Thomas H. Fletcher Damage two hundred & fifty dollars & therefore he sues and therin pledges &c

Douglass Atto. prosque.

And the said Defendant comes & defends the wrongs & injury when &c where &c and craves aye of the writing obligatory & it is read to him and of the endorsements thereon and they are read to him in the words & figures following viz this 11th of February 1818 then received of the within note ninety five dollars & one cent.

John Hallum

which being read & heard said defendant saith he paid the said debt in said decleration mentioned in part to said John Hallum after it became due & payable & before said writing obligatory was endorsed by him & that he paid the residue of said debt to John P. Erwen & Co after it became due & payable & before said writing obligatory or bill single was endorsed by them & this he is ready to verify whereupon he prays judgement &c.

W. Williams, for Deft.

Replication & issue

Douglass atto. for Plft.

And now at this term (to wit) the term first above mentioned came the parties by their attornies & thereupon came a jury of good and lawful men (to wit) Reuben Rider, Samuel Mothsral, Jacob Vantrice, William Stafford, David Billings, James Ross, Henry Carson, Simpson Organ, Jacob H. Thomas, Peter Raglin, Silas Chapman, & Joseph Cole, who being elected tried and sworn the truth to speak upon the issue joined upon their oaths do say they find for the plaintiff the balance of his debt amounting to eleven hundred & fifty two dollars & thirteen cents and assess his damage by the detention of said debt to one hundred & twenty eight ___ & eighty six cents It is there fore considered by the Court that the said plaintiff (P-207) plaintiff recover against of said defendant the balance of his debt and damages amounting to twelve hundred dollars & ninety nine cents as by the jurors aforesaid in form aforesaid assessed and also his costs about his suit in this behalf expended From which judgement the Defendant prays an appeal to the next Circuit Court to be holden for the County of Wilson at the Court - in Lebanon on the fourth Monday in October next and entered into bond as the law directs - with John Hallum and James Slate, his securities filed reasons &c and there upon an appeal is granted.

```
    Bill of Costs
writ, tax & bond 302½  1 continuance 40¢  1 spa. 20.  Indt. 100 cts
    transcript and seal 140                                $6.02½
Sheff. arrest & bond  125 cts. 1 spa.  25¢ empannel-
ing jury  16.                                             1.66
Atto. Douglass                                            2.50
M. Davis  a witness                                       1.50
                                                        $ 11.68½
```

(P-208) Pleas before the Court of pleas and quarter sessions began and held for the County of Wilson at the Court house in the town of Lebanon on Monday the 1st day of November 1819 & 44 year of American Independence.

Tuesday morning Court met according to adjournment Present the worshipful William Steele, Walter Caruth, Joseph T. Williams, Ransom Gwyn, esquires who took their seats & proceeded to business,

```
JOHN CARTWRIGHT   PLFT. )
        VS.           )  In Debt.
JOHN FISHER       DEFT. )
```

Be it remembered that heretofore (to wit) on the 27th day of April 1819 John Fisher was attached to answer John Cartwright on a plea that he render to him the sum of twenty four hundred & five dollars & eighty two cents which to him he owes and from him he unjustly detains to his damage five hundred dollars –

At May Term 1819 came the plaintiff by his attorney Saml Houston Esqr. and filed his decleration in the words & figures following (to wit)

```
STATE OF TENNESSEE )  Court of
WILSON COUNTY      )  Pleas & quarter sessions  May term 1819  viz.
```

John Cartwright by his attorney Complains of John Fisher, in Custody &c in a plea that he render to him the sum of twenty four hundred and five dollars & eighty two cents, which to him he owes and from him unjustly detains For that whereas the said John Fisher by the name and subscription of John Fisher made his certain bill single sealed with his seal dated the 10th of November 1818 (to wit) At Lebanon in the County of Wilson aforesaid and thereby promised to pay John Cartwright the sum of twenty four hundred & five dollars and eighty two cents, on or before the 7th day of January next after the date there of for value received and the bill single of that day and date is here ready to be produced to the Court whereby in action hath accured to the said John Cartwright to ask and demand the said sum of money in the said bill mentioned ~~in the said bill mentioned~~ nevertheless the said John Fisher altho often requested to pay the said sum of twenty four hundred and five dollars & eighty two cents by the said John Cartwright hath never yet paid the same (P-209) nor any part thereof to the said John Cartwright, but to pay the same or any part thereof he the said John Fisher hath hitherto wholly refused and still refuses to the damage of the said John Cartwright. therefore he sues, & these are by pledges &c

Sam Houston, Atto.
for Plaintiff

The defendant pleads payment

S. Anderson, Atto for Defendant

Replication and issue At August Term 1819, the rule of Court, Continued at November Term 1819 Came the parties aforesaid by their attornies and thereupon came a jury of good and lawful men(to wit) Isham Morris, Geo. Williamson, Wm. M. Swan, Geo. M. Smith, Geo. L. Smith, Thos. B. Baker, Arden Somers, Wm New, John M. Jackson, Everett Mitchell, Wm Thomas & William Petway, who being elected tried and sworn the truth the truth to speak upon the issue joined upon their oaths do say they find that the defendant has not paid the balance of the debt in the plaintiff decleration mentioned of nine hundred and eighty six dollars & fifty eight cents, and assess the Plaintiff damage by reason there of to ninety one dollars & sixty eight cents.

It is therefore considered by the Court that the said plaintiff recover against the said defendant the balance of his debt aforesaid, with the damages aforesaid by the jurors aforesaid assessed, amounting in the whole to one thousand & seventy eight dollars & twenty six cents, and also his cost about his suit in this behalf expended & from which judgement the defendant prays an appeal to the next Circuit Court to be held at Lebanon on the fourth Monday in April next.

Filed reasons entered into bond as the law directs and thereupon an appeal is granted.

Bill of Costs.

writ law tax & bond -----	$30\frac{1}{2}$
one Continuance 40 Indt. 100	140
Sheffs. arrest and bond 125 calling cause & jury 16	141
Attorney	250
Transcript & seal	140
	$9.73\frac{1}{2}$

(P-210)

JAMES WRIGHT PLAINTIFF)
VS) In Debt.
JOHN & MORRIS HALLUM)
DEFT.)

Be it remembered that heretofore (to wit) on the 13th day of May 1819 John Hallum & Morris Hallum, were attached to answer James Wright of a plea that they render unto him one hundred and twenty five dollars which to him they owe & from him unjustly detains to his damage fifty dollars.

At August term 1819 the plaintiff by his attorney James Rucks Esquire came into Court and filed his declaration in the words & figures following (to wit)

WILSON COUNTY) August Session
STATE OF TENNESSEE) County Court 1819

James Wright by his attorney Complains of John Hallum & Morris Hallum in Custody of the Sheriff &c of a plea that they render unto him the said James one hundred and twenty five dollars which to him they owe and from him unjustly detain.

For that whereas on the 5th day of February 1818 at Lebanon in the County aforesaid, the said John and the said Morriss by their certain writing obligatory sealed with their seals unto the Court here now shewn, bearing date the same day and year aforesaid bound themselves twelve months after the date of the said writing obligatory to pay to him the said James the aforesaid sum of one hundred and twenty five dollars with interest from the date of the said writing obligatory, if not punctually paid, for value received, yet the said John and the said Morriss did not pay twelve months after the date of the said writing obligatory to the said James the aforesaid sum of one hundred and twenty five dollars nor any part thereof nor have they at any time hither to paid the same, with interest from the date of the said wording obligatory tho often requested but to pay the said sum of money to the said James they the said John & the said Morris have hither to wholly refused and still doth refuse to the damage of the said James of fifty dollars.

Wherefore he brings his suit

James Bucks atto. for plaintiff

Plea payment set off.

S. Houston atto. for Deft

Replication & issue

(P-211)   At November term 1819 came the parties aforesaid by their attornies, and thereupon came a jury of good and lawful men (to wit) Isham Morris, George Williamson, William M. Swain, George M. Smith, George L. Smith, Thomas B. Baker, Ardin Sommers, William New, John M. Jackson, Everett Mitchell, William Thomas, & William Petway, who being elected tried and sworn the truth to speak upon the issue joined upon their oaths do say they find that the Defendants have not paid the debt in the plaintiff declaration mentioned of one hundred and twenty five dollars as the plaintiff in replying hath alledged and do assess the plaintiff damage by reason thereof to five dollars.

It is therefore considered by the Court that the said plaintiff recover against the said defendant his debt aforesaid, to gether with the damages aforesaid by the jurors aforesaid in form aforesaid assessed amounting in the whole to one hundred and thirty dollars also his costs by him about his suit in this be half expended &c

From which judgement the defendants pray an appeal to the next Circuit Court to be held for the County of Wilson at the Court house in Lebanon on the fourth Monday in April next and upon their entering into bond as the law directs and filing reasons an appeal is granted them.

Bill of Costs

writ law tax & bond - - - - - -	302½
One Continuance 40¢ Judgement 100¢	140
Sheff. two arrest & bond - - - -	225
Calling Cause & jury	16
Attorney Bucks	250
Transcript & seal	140
Doll.	10.73½

(P-212)   Pleas &c.

```
MCNEIL FISK & RUTHERFORD  PLFT.)
        VS.                     )
GEORGE HALLUM    DEFT.          ) In Debt.
```

Be it remembered that heretofore (to wit) on the 15th day of May 1819 George Hallum was attached to answer Nathaniel McNeil, James Fisk & William Rutherford assignees and merchants in trade trading under the character of McNeil Fisk & Rutherford in a plea that he render to them the sum of three hundred and eight dollars which to them he owes & from them unjustly detains to their damage one hundred dollars.

At August term 1819 Came the plaintiff by their attornies Douglass, & Stoddert and filed their declaration in the words and figures following (to-wit)

```
STATE OF TENNESSEE ) Court of pleas & quarter sessions
WILSON COUNTY      ) AUGUST term 1819
```

Nathaniel McNeil, James Fisk & William Rutherford assignees, merchants, and partners in trade trading under the style & character of McNeil Fisk, & Rutherford by their attornies Complain of George Hallum in Custody &c in a plea that he render to them three hundred and eight dollars which to them he owes & from him unjustly detains For that where as at Nashville (to wit) at Lebanon in the County aforesaid the said George Hallum, by the name & description of G. Hallum made his certain bill single sealed with the seal dated July 23rd 1818 and thereby promised to pay John P. Erwin, & Co. three hundred and eight dollars for value received nine months after the date thereof and the said bill single of that day and date, is here ready to be produced to the Court, and whereas afterwards (to wit) on the __ day of ___ 1818 at Lebanon in the County aforesaid the said bill single was assigned, by the said John P. Erwin, & Co to the firm of Erwen, McLaughlin & Co by the written indorsement and signature of the said John P. Erwen & Co before said bill single or any part thereof was paid or due and the said John P. Erwin, & Co then and there delivered the said bill single so indorsed to the said firm of Erwen, McLaughlin & Co. and the said Erwen McLaughlin & Co. to whom or to whose order the payment of the said sum of money contained in the said bill single was to be made afterwards & before the payment of the said sum of money or any part (P-213) thereof (to wit) on the first day of September 1818 at Lebanon in the County aforesaid indorsed the said bill single their own proper hands being thereon subscribed and by that indorsement appointed the contents of the said bill single to be paid to the said firm of McNeil Fisk, and Rutherford, of which said indorsements, so made on the said note as aforesaid the said George Hallum afterwards (to wit) on the __ day of ___ 1818 at Lebanon in the County aforesaid then and there had notice by reason whereof and by force of the Acts of the general assembly in such case made and provided a right accrued to the said McNeil, Fisk & Rutherford to ask and have of the said George Hallum, the said sum of money in said bill single mentioned.

Nevertheless the said George Hallum refuses to pay the same to the said McNeil Fisk & Rutherford, nor have they received any part thereof from the said George Hallum by non payment whereof the said firm of McNeil Fisk & Rutherford have sustained damage to the amount of ___ dollars and therefore they sue & therefore pledges &c

Douglass, & Stoddert Pro-que.

Plea payment & setoff

Houston Atto. for Deft.

At November term 1819 came the parties aforesaid by their attornies and thereupon came a jury of good and lawful men (to wit) Isham Morriss, George Williamson, William M. Swain, George M. Smith, George L. Smith, Thomas B. Baker, Ardin Sommers, William New, John M. Jackson, Everett Mitchell, William Thomas, & William Petway, who being elected tried and sworn the truth to speak upon the issue joined upon their oaths do say they find the defendant has not paid the debt in the plaintiffs decleration mentioned of three hundred and eight dollars, and assess the plaintiffs damage by by reason thereof to nine dollars & fifty cents It is therefore considered by the Court that the said Plaintiff recover against the said defendant the debt aforesaid with the damages aforesaid by the jurors aforesaid assessed amounting in the whole to three hundred and seventeen dollars & fifty cents. and also their cost about ~~their costs about~~ their suit in this behalf expended. From which judgement the said Defendant prays an appeal to the next Circuit Court to be held for the County of Wilson at the Court house in Lebanon on the fourth Monday in April next and upon entering into bond & filing reasons as the law directs an appeal is hereby granted.

(P-214) Bill of Costs

writ, law tax & bond - - - - -	302½
Appeal bond 60 Judgement 100	160
Transcript & seal	140
Sheff. Arrest	100
Attornies Douglass & Stoddert	250
Dolls	9.52½

Pleas &c.

GEORGE SMITH ASSEE PLFT.)
       VS.   ) In Debt.
JOHN FISHER   DEFT.   )

Be it remembered that heretofore (to wit) on the 20th day of July 1819 John Fisher was attached to answer George Smith assignee of Stump & Cox of a plea that he render to him five hundred & forty three dollars, which to him he owes and from him unjustly detains to his damage one hundred dollars.

At August term 1819 came the plaintiff by his atto's.and filed his declaration in the words & figures following viz.

STATE OF TENNESSEE   ) Court of pleas & quarter sessions
WILSON COUNTY   ) August term 1819 viz

George Smith assigned of Stump & Cox by atto. Complains of John Fisher in Custody &c in a plea that he render to him five hundred and forty three dollars which to him he owes and from him unjustly detains, for that whereas at Nashville (to wit) At Lebanon in the County aforesaid John Fisher, by the name & description of John Fisher made his certain bill single sealed with his seal dated March 24th 1818 & thereby promised to pay to the firm of Stump & Cox five hundred and forty three dollars ten months after date thereof, for value received, and the said bill single of that day and date is here ready to be produced to the Court, and the said firm of Stump & Cox to whom the payment of the said sum of money contained in the said bill single was to be made afterwards and before the payment of the said sum of money or of any part thereof and before the same was due (to wit) on the ___ day of ___ 181 at Lebanon in the County aforesaid indorsed the said bill single their own proper hands being thereon subscribed and by that indorsement appointed the contents of the said bill single to be paid to the said George Smith of which said (P-215) indorsement the said John Fisher, afterwards (to wit) in the ___ day of ____ 18___ at Lebanon in the County aforesaid then & there had notice by reason whereof a right accrued to the said George Smith to ask and have of the said John Fisher the said sum of money in said bill single mentioned nevertheless the said John Fisher refuses to pay the same to the said George Smith nor has he received any part thereof from the said John Fisher by non payment whereof the said George Smith has sustained damage to the amount of ___ dollars and therefore he sues & there are pledges &c.

                              Douglass & Stoddert   Pro que.

Plea payment replication & issue   set off report & issue.

                         Anderson. atto for Deft.

At November term 1819 came the parties aforesaid by their attornies and thereupon Came a jury of good and lawful men (to wit) Beverly Williams, Bennett Babb, Jesse Bowers, Charles Locke, William Terver, Thomas Hearn, John Rhea, Henry Shannon, John Calhoon, James Law, John Foster, & William Carruth, who being elected tried and sworn the truth to speak upon the issue joined upon their oaths do say they find the defendant has not paid the balance of the debt in the plaintiffs declaration mentioned of four hundred and fifteen dollars & seventy one cents and do assess the plaintiffs damage by reason of the detention of his debt to eighteen dollars It is therefore considered by the Court that the said Plaintiff recover against the said defendant the debt aforesaid to-gether with his damages aforesaid by the jurors aforesaid assessed and also his costs about his suit in this behalf expended, From which judgement the defendant prays an appeal to the next Circuit Court to be held at the Court house in Lebanon on the fourth Monday in April next, and upon his entering into bond as the law directs & filing reasons an appeal is here granted.

        Bill of Costs.

    Writ Law tax & bond - - - -   302½
    Appeal bond 60¢ Continuance 40¢   1.00

Judgement	1 00
Transcript & Seal	1 40
Sheff. Arrest & bond	1 25
Attornies Douglass & Stoddert	2 50
Dolls.	10.17½